Aug. 11, 2010

Say It
Right in
DUTCH

Easily Pronounced Language Systems

Clyde Peters

New York   Chicago   San Francisco   Lisbon   London   Madrid   Mexico City
Milan   New Delhi   San Juan   Seoul   Singapore   Sydney   Toronto

Library of Congress Cataloging-in-Publication Data

Say it right in Dutch / Easily Pronounced Language Systems ; author: Clyde Peters ;
    illustrations: Luc Nisset.
           p.   cm. — (Say it right)
        Text in English and Dutch.
        Includes index.
        ISBN 0-07-170140-0 (alk. paper)
          1. Dutch language—Pronunciation.   2. Dutch language—Spoken Dutch.
        3. Dutch language—Conversation and phrase books—English.   I. Peters, Clyde
        (Clyde Elias)   II. Nisset. Luc.   III. Easily Pronounced Language Systems.
        IV. Title.

        PF121.S235   2009
        439.318'2421—dc22

                                                                2009039808

1 2 3 4 5 6 7 8 9 10 11 12 13 14 15   WFR/WFR   1 9 8 7 6 5 4 3 2 1 0

ISBN 978-0-07-170140-2
MHID   0-07-170140-0

Also available: *Say It Right in Arabic* • *Say It Right in Brazilian Portuguese* • *Say It Right
in Chinese* • *Say It Right in Chinese, Audio Edition* • *Say It Right in French* • *Say It Right
in French, Audio Edition* • *Say It Right in German* • *Say It Right in Greek* • *Say It Right in
Italian* • *Say It Right in Italian, Audio Edition* • *Say It Right in Japanese* • *Say It Right in
Korean* • *Say It Right in Russian* • *Say It Right in Spanish* • *Say It Right in Spanish, Audio
Edition* • *Say It Right in Thai* • *Dígalo correctamente en inglés [Say It Right in English]*

Author: Clyde Peters
Illustrations: Luc Nisset
President, EPLS: Betty Chapman, www.isayitright.com
Senior Series Editor: Priscilla Leal Bailey
Dutch Language Consultants: Marcel Hoogeveen and Nathalie Yfs

CONTENTS

INTRODUCTION

The SAY IT RIGHT FOREIGN LANGUAGE PHRASE BOOK SERIES has been developed with the conviction that learning to speak a foreign language should be fun and easy!

All SAY IT RIGHT phrase books feature the EPLS Vowel Symbol System, a revolutionary phonetic system that stresses consistency, clarity, and above all, simplicity!

Since this unique phonetic system is used in all SAY IT RIGHT phrase books, you only have to learn the VOWEL SYMBOL SYSTEM ONCE!

The SAY IT RIGHT series uses the easiest phrases possible for English speakers to pronounce, and is designed to reflect how foreign languages are used by native speakers.

You will be amazed at how confidence in your pronunciation leads to an eagerness to talk to other people in their own language.

Whether you want to learn a new language for travel, education, business, study, or personal enrichment, SAY IT RIGHT phrase books offer a simple and effective method of pronunciation and communication.

PRONUNCIATION GUIDE

Most English speakers are familiar with the Dutch word **Dike (Dijk).** This is how the correct pronunciation is represented in the EPLS Vowel Symbol System.

All Dutch vowel sounds are assigned a specific non-changing symbol. When these symbols are used in conjunction with consonants and read normally, pronunciation of even the most difficult foreign word becomes incredibly EASY!

On the following page are all the EPLS Vowel Symbols used in this book. They are EASY to LEARN since their sounds are familiar. Beneath each symbol are three English words which contain the sound of the symbol.

Practice pronouncing the words under each symbol until you mentally associate the correct vowel sound with the correct symbol. Most symbols are pronounced the way they look!

THE SAME BASIC SYMBOLS ARE USED IN ALL SAY IT RIGHT PHRASE BOOKS!

EPLS VOWEL SYMBOL SYSTEM

Ⓐ
Ace
Bake
Safe

ⒺⒺ
See
Feet
Meet

Ⓘ
Ice
Kite
Pie

Ⓞ
Oak
Cold
Sold

ⓞⓞ
Cool
Pool
Too

ⓐ̆
Cat
Hat
Sad

ⓔ̆
Men
Red
Bed

ⓐⓗ
Calm
Hot
Off

ⓘ
Win
Sit
Give

ⓞⓦ
Cow
How
Now

ⓞⓨ
Boy
Toy
Joy

Ⓤr
Hurt
Turn
Burn

ⓞⓤ
Could
Would
Should

ⓔⓦ
New
Few
View

Note: When you see an elongated symbol it is a reminder to slightly lengthen the sound you make.

EPLS CONSONANTS

Consonants are letters like **T**, **D**, and **K**. They are easy to recognize and their pronunciation seldom changes. The following pronunciation guide letters represent some Dutch consonants and their EPLS equivalents.

These **EPLS** letters/symbols represent the Dutch letters **g**, **ch**, and **ig**.

In written Dutch the **g** is rarely pronounced as in English. Its correct sound is guttural as in the Scottish word lo**ch** and is represented by H̰. The tilde beneath indicates that the guttural sound is dragged out. The EPLS Vowel Symbols ⓤ̰ and ⓐ̰ are also shown with the tilde beneath because the **h** within the symbol should be guttural and dragged out. The **ch** letter combination is guttural and is represented by K̰ and sounds similar to a dragged **k** sound. The **ig** letter combination is guttural and is represented by EPLS ⓤ̰.

R̰   Pronounce this EPLS letter like the rolled Spanish **r**.

TS   Pronounce these letters like the **ts** in the English word hi**ts**.

ZH   Pronounce these letters like **s** in the English word mea**s**ure.

PRONUNCIATION TIPS

- Each pronunciation guide word is broken into syllables. Read each word slowly, one syllable at a time, increasing speed as you become more familiar with the system.

- In Dutch it is important to emphasize certain syllables. This mark (´) over the syllable reminds you to STRESS that syllable.

- In the spoken language, the pronunciation of a particular letter will be affected by the letters in front of it or directly following.

- This phrase book provides a means to speak and be understood in Dutch. To perfect your Dutch accent you must listen closely to Dutch speakers and adjust your speech accordingly.

- The pronunciation choices in this book were chosen for their simplicity and effectiveness.

ICONS USED IN THIS BOOK

KEY WORDS

You will find this icon at the beginning of chapters indicating key words relating to chapter content. These are important words to become familiar with.

PHRASEMAKER

The Phrasemaker icon provides the traveler with a choice of phrases that allows the user to make his or her own sentences.

Say It
Right in
DUTCH

ESSENTIAL WORDS AND PHRASES

Here are some basic words and phrases that will help you express your needs and feelings in **Dutch**.

Hi

Hoi

H⊚y

Hello

Hallo (polite)

H⊚-L⊚

How are you?

Hoe gaat het?

H⊚ H⊚T H⊚T

Fine, thank you

Goed, dank je

H⊚T D⊚NK-Y⊚

And you?

En jij?

⊚N Y⊚

Good morning

Goedemorgen

HOO-Duh MOR-Huhn

Good afternoon

Goede middag

HOO-Duh MI-Dah

Good evening

Goede avond

HOO-Duh ah-VONT

Good night

Goedenacht

HOO-Duh NahKT

Mr. and Sir

Meneer

Muh-NEER

Mrs.

Mevrouw

Muh-FRow

Miss

Juffrouw

Yuhf-FRow

See you later

Tot ziens

TOT SEENS

Good-bye

Dag

DahH

Bye

Doei

DOOEE

Used more often with people you know, but can be used in a casual, friendly way, much like the Hawaiian word "aloha." You will hear this everywhere in Amsterdam.

Yes

Ja

Y(ah)

No

Nee

N(A)

Please

Alstublieft

(ah)LS-T(oo)-BL(EE)'FT

Thank you very much. (formal)

Dank u wel.

D(ah)'NK (oo) V(e)L

Thank you very much. (informal)

Dank je wel.

D(ah)'NK Y(uh) V(e)L

Thanks (very formal)

Dank u

D(ah)'NK (oo)

Excuse me / I'm sorry

Pardon

P(ah)R-D(O)'N

I don't understand!

Ik begrijp het niet!

ⒾK Bⓤⓗ-HⓇⒾP Hⓔⓣ NⒺⒺT

Do you understand?

Berijpt u?

Bⓤⓗ-HⓇⒾPT ⓄⓄ

I'm a tourist.

Ik ben een toerist.

ⒾK BⓔN ⓤⓗN TⓄⓄ-ⓇⒾST

I don't understand Dutch.

Ik begrijp geen Nederlands.

ⒾK Bⓤⓗ-HⓇⒾP HⒶN
NⒶ-DⓊⓡ-LⒶⓗNDS

Do you speak English?

Spreekt u Engels?

SPⓇⒶKT ⓄⓄ ⒶN-GⓤⓗLZ

Please repeat.

Wilt u dat herhalen?

VⒾLT ⓄⓄ DⓐⓗT HⒺⓇ-Hⓐⓗ-LⓤⓗN

FEELINGS

I would like...

Ik wil graag...

ⒾK VⒾL H℟⒜H...

I want...

Ik wil...

ⒾK VⒾL...

I have...

Ik heb...

ⒾK HⓔB...

I know.

Ik weet het.

ⒾK Vⓐ T Hⓔ T

I don't know.

Ik weet het niet.

ⒾK Vⓐ T Hⓔ T
Nⓔ T

I like it.

Ik vind het leuk.

ⒾK FⒾNT Hⓔ T LⓞⓤK

I don't like it.

Ik vind het niet leuk.

ⒾK FⒾNT Hⓔ T Nⓔ T LⓞⓤK

I'm lost.

Ik ben verdwaald.

ⒾK BⓔN FⓊʳRT-VⓐⱨLT

We are lost.

Wij zijn verdwaald.

VⒾ ZⒾN FⓊʳRT-VⓐⱨLT

I'm ill.

Ik ben ziek.

ⒾK BⓔN ZⒺⒺK

I think so.

Dat denk ik.

DⓐⱨT DⓔNK ⒾK

I think...

Volgens mij...

FⓄ́L-ⱨⓊⱨNS MⒾ...

I'm hungry.

Ik heb honger.

ⒾK HⓔB HⓄ́N-ⱨⓊʳ

INTRODUCTIONS

Use the following phrases when meeting someone for the first time, both privately or in business.

My name is...

Ik heet ...

ⒾK H④T...

What's your name?

Hoe heet je?

H⑩ H④T Yⓤ

Nice to meet you.

Leuk je te ontmoeten.

Lⓞ︎K Yⓤ Tⓤ ⓄNT-Mⓞ︎-Tⓤ︎N

GENERAL GUIDELINES

The Netherlands is a densely populated country. It is popular for its windmills, tulips, cheese, clogs, and bicycles. It is also well known for its social tolerance. The Dutch have a code of etiquette that governs social behavior and is considered very important.

- When introducing themselves, the Dutch shake hands and say their name (first and/or surname).

- The handshake is firm and swift, accompanied by a smile.

- Usually an acquaintance will introduce a visitor to others, otherwise, the guest introduces himself.

- The Dutch consider it rude not to identify oneself.

- The Dutch expect eye contact while speaking with someone.

THE BIG QUESTIONS

Who?

Wie?

V☉

Who is it?

Wie is het?

V☉ ①S H☉T

What?

Wat?

V☉T

What's that?

Wat is dat?

V☉T ①S D☉T

When?

Waneer?

V☉-N☉R

Where?

Waar?

V☉R

Where is…?

Waar is...?

V@hR ⓘS...

Which?

Welke?

V@̃L-K@h

Why?

Waarom?

V@h̀-R@@M

How?

Hoe?

H@@

How much? / How many?

Hoeveel?

H@@-V@́L

How long will it take?

Hoe long duurt het?

H@@ L@hNG D@@RT H@̃T

ASKING FOR THINGS

The following phrases are valuable for directions, food, help, etc.

I would like...

Ik wil graag...

ⒾK VⒾL HRⓐⓗ...

I need...

Ik heb...nodig

ⒾK HⒺB (...) NⓄ-DⓊⓗ

Can you...?

Kunt u...?

KⓄⓊNT ⓄⓄ...

When asking a question it is polite to say "May I ask" and "Thank you."

May I ask?	**Thank you**
Mag ik vragen?	Dank u wel
MⓐⓗH ⒾK FRⓐⓗ-HⓊⓗN	DⓐⓗN-KⓄⓄ VⒺL

PHRASEMAKER

I would like…

Ik wil graag...

ⒾK VⒾL HRⓐH...

▸ **more coffee**

meer koffie

MⒺⒺR KⓄ-FⒺⒺ

▸ **some water**

wat water

VⓐT Vⓐ-TⓊr

▸ **some ice**

wat ijs

VⓐT ⒾS

▸ **the menu**

het menu

HⒺT MⒺ-Nⓞⓞ

PHRASEMAKER

Here are a few sentences
you can use when you feel
the urge to say **I need**... or **can you**...?

I need...

Ik heb ...

ⒾK HⓔB...

▸ **your help**

uw hulp nodig

ⓔⓦ HⓔLP NⓄ-Dⓤⓗ

▸ **more money**

meer geld nodig

MⒺⒺR HⓔLT NⓄ-Dⓤⓗ

▸ **change** (money)

klein geld nodig

KLⒾ N HⓔLT NⓄ-Dⓤⓗ

▸ **a doctor**

een dokter nodig

ⓤⓗN DⓄK-TⓊr NⓄ-Dⓤⓗ

▸ **a lawyer**

een advocaat nodig

ⓤⓗN ⓐⓗD-VⓄ-Kⓐⓗ NⓄ-Dⓤⓗ

PHRASEMAKER

Can you…

Kunt u...

K@NT @...

▶ **help me?**

mij helpen?

M① H@L-P@N

▶ **give me?**

mij geven?

M① H@-F@N

▶ **tell me…?**

mij vertelen...?

M① F@R-T@-L@N ...

▶ **take me to…?**

mij naar ... brengen?

M① N@B (...) BR@N-G@N

ASKING THE WAY

No matter how independent you are, sooner or later you'll probably have to ask for directions.

Where is…?

Waar is…?

V@ⓗR ⒾS…

I'm looking for…

Ik zoek…

ⒾK Z◎K…

Is it near?

Is het dichtbij?

ⒾS Hⓔ̃T   D◎K̓T-BⒾ

Is it far?

Is het ver?

ⒾS Hⓔ̃T Fⓔ̃R

Left	**Right**
Links	Rechts
Lⓔ̃NKS	Rⓔ̃K̓T

PHRASEMAKER

Where is…?

Waar is...?

V@B ①S...

▸ **the restroom?**

de toilet?

D@ TW@-L@T

▸ **the telephone?**

de telefoon?

D@ T@-L@-F@N

▸ **the beach?**

het strand?

H@T STR@NT

▸ **the hotel?**

het hotel?

H@T H@-T@L

▸ **the train for...?**

de trein voor…?

D@ TR@N F@R...

TIME

What time is it?

Hoe laat is het?

H⃝OO L⃝ahT ⃝IS H⃝ēT

Morning

Ochtend

⃝OK-T⃝ēNT

Noon

Middag

M⃝I-D⃝ah

Night

Nacht

N⃝ahKT

Today

Vandaag

F⃝ahN-D⃝ah

Tomorrow

Morgen

M⃝OR-H⃝uhN

This week

Deze week

DA-Suh VAK

This month

Deze maand

DA-Suh MahNT

This year

Dit jaar

DiT YahB

Now

Nu

Noo

Later

Later

Lah-TUr

Never

Nooit

NoyT

WHO IS IT?

I

Ik

ⒾK

You	**You** (informal)
Jij	Je
YⒾ	Yⓤⓗ

You (formal)

U

⓪⓪

He / She / It

Hij / Zij / Het

HⒾ / SⒾ / Hⓔ̈T

We

Wij

Vⓞⓤ

They

Zij

ZⒾ

THIS AND THAT

The equivalents of **this, that,** and **these** are as follows:

This

Dit

DⒾT

This is mine.

Dit is mijn.

DⒾT ⒾS MⒾN

That

Dat

DⓐⓗT

That is mine.

Dat is mijn.

DⓐⓗT ⒾS MⒾN

These

Deze

DⒶ'-Sⓤⓗ

These are mine.

Deze zijn mijn.

DⒶ'-Sⓤⓗ ZⒾN MⒾN

USEFUL OPPOSITES

Near	Far
Dichtbij	Ver
D(i)KT-B(i)	F(e)R

Here	There
Hier	Daar
H(ee)R	D(ah)R

Left	Right
Links	Recht
L(e)NKS	R(e)KT

More	Less
Meer	Minder
M(ee)R	M(i)N-D(ur)

Big	Small
Groot	Klein
HR(ow)T	KL(i)N

Open	**Closed**
Open	Gesloten
Ⓞ-Pⓤɴ	Hⓤ-SLⓄ-Tⓤɴ

Cheap	**Expensive**
Goedkoop	Duur
HⓞⓞT-Kⓞ̶P	Dⓞⓞʀ

Dirty	**Clean**
Vies	Schoon
FⓔⓔS	SHⓄɴ

Good	**Bad**
Goed	Slecht
HⓞⓞT	SLⓔKT

Vacant	**Occupied**
Vrij	Bezet
FʀⒾ	Bⓤ-Zⓔ̈T

Right	**Wrong**
Goed	Fout
HⓞⓞT	FⓞⱳT

WORDS OF ENDEARMENT

I like you.

Je bent aardig.

Y⒰ B⒠NT ⒜'R-D⒰

I love you.

Ik hou van jou.

⒤K H⒰ F⒜N Y⒰

I love Amsterdam.

Ik hou van Amsterdam.

⒤K H⒰ F⒜N ⒜'M-ST⒰R-D⒜M

My friend (to a male)

Mijn vriend

M⒤N FR⒠NT

My friend (to a female)

Mijn vriendin

M⒤N FR⒠'N-D⒤N

Kiss me!

Kus me!

K⒰S M⒰

WORDS OF ANGER

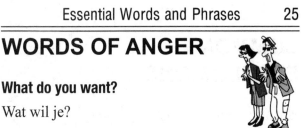

What do you want?

Wat wil je?

V@hT V(i)L Y(uh)

Leave me alone!

Laat me met rust!

L@hT M(uh) M(e)T R(ou)ST

Go away!

Ga weg!

H@h V(e)H

Be quiet!

Wees stil!

V@S ST(i)L

That's enough!

Het is genoeg!

H(e)T (i)S H(uh)-N(oo)H

COMMON EXPRESSIONS

When you are at a loss for words but have the feeling you should say something, try one of these!

Have a safe journey!

Goede reis!

H͟oo-Duh Ris

Bless you! (after someone sneezes)

Gezondheid!

H͟e-ZON-TiT

Sure!

Zeker!

SA-KUr

What's happening?

Wat gebeurt er?

VahT Huh-BUrT Ur

Have fun!

Veel plezier!

FeeL PLe-SeeR

A toast!

Proost!

PROOST

Good luck!

Veel geluk!

FAL HUH-LOOK

Happy dreams!

Welterusten!

VEL-TUr-STUHN

What a shame!

Dat is zonde!

DAHT IS SON-DUH

Well done!

Goed gedaan!

HOOT HUH-DAHN

Bravo!

Bravo!

BRAH-VO

True

Waar

VAHR

USEFUL COMMANDS

Stop!   (Same as in English)

Ho!

H⊙

Go!

Ga!

H͟ah

Wait!

Wacht!

Vah KT

Hurry!

Schnel!

SHNĕLP

Slow down!

Langzaam aan!

Lah NG-Sah M   ah N

Come here!

Kom hier!

KⓄM   HⓔⓔR

EMERGENCIES

Fire!

Brand!

BR**ah**NT

Help!

Help!

H**e**LP

Emergency!

Noodgeval!

N**o**T-H**uh**-V**ah**L

Call the police!

Bel de politie!

B**e**L D**uh** P**o**-L**ee**T-S**ee**

Call an ambulance!

Bel een ambulance!

B**e**L **uh**N **ah**M-B**oo**-L**ah**N-TS**uh**

ARRIVAL

Passing through customs should be easy since there are usually agents available who speak English. You may be asked how long you intend to stay and if you have anything to declare.

- Have your passport ready.

- All visitors require a passport

- Be sure all documents are up to date.

- While in Holland, it is wise to keep receipts for everything you buy.

- If you have connecting flights, be sure to reconfirm in advance and arrive 2 to 3 hours early for flights and lengthy customs processing.

- Make sure your luggage is clearly marked inside and out and always keep an eye on it when in public places.

- It is always important to keep a basic inventory of items you have packed and checked due to the unfortunate possibility that your luggage may be lost.

- Keep in mind that many airlines will not reimburse you for lost jewelry.

KEY WORDS

Baggage

Bagage

B@-H@-SH@

Customs

Douane

D@@-N@

Documents

Documenten

D@-K@-M@N-T@N

Passport

Paspoort

P@S-P@RT

Porter

Hotelbediende

H@-T@L B@-D@N-D@

Taxi

Taxi

T@K-S@

USEFUL PHRASES

Here is my passport.

Hier is mijn paspoort.

HEER ÕS MÕN Pah'S-PORT

I have nothing to declare.

Ik heb niets om aan te geven.

ÕK HĕB NEETS ÕM
ahN Tuh HA'-fuhN

I'm here on business.

Ik ben hier voor zaken.

ÕK BĕN HEER FOOR Sah'-KuhN

I'm on vacation.

Ik ben op vakantie.

ÕK BĕN ÕP Fah'-Kah'N-SEE

Is there a problem?

Is er een probleem?

ÕS ĕR uhN PRO'-BLahM

PHRASEMAKER

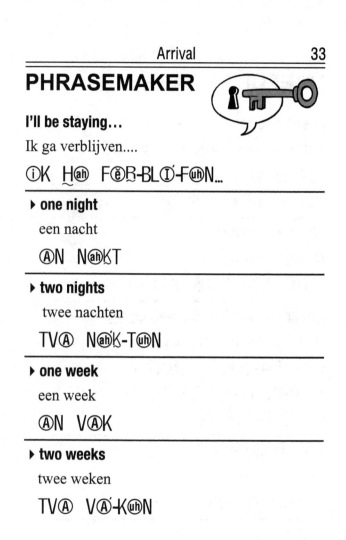

I'll be staying...

Ik ga verblijven....

ⓘK H͜ⓐⓗ FⓔR-BLⓘ-FⓤⓗN...

▸ **one night**

een nacht

ⓐN NⓐⓗKT

▸ **two nights**

twee nachten

TVⓐ NⓐⓗK-TⓤⓗN

▸ **one week**

een week

ⓐN Vⓐ K

▸ **two weeks**

twee weken

TVⓐ Vⓐ-KⓤⓗN

USEFUL PHRASES

I need a porter.

Ik heb een hotelbediende nodig.

ⒾK HⒺB ⓤⒽN HO-TⒺL
Bⓐ⒣-DⒺⒺN-DⓤⒽ NO-Dⓤ͜

These are my bags.

Dit zijn mijn koffers.

DⒾT ZⒾN MⒾN KⓄF-FⓊⓇS

Please can you help me with my luggage?

Alstublieft kunt u mij helpen met mijn bagage?

ⓐ⒣L-STⓄⓄ-BLⒺⒺFT KⓄⓤNT
ⓄⓄ MⒾ HⒺL-PⓤⒽN MⒺT
MⒾN Bⓐ⒣-Hⓐ⒣-SHⓤⒽ

I'm missing a bag.

Ik mis een koffer.

ⒾK MⒾS ⓤⒽN KⓄF-FⓊr

Thank you. This is for you.

Dank je wel. Dit is voor u.

Dⓐ⒣NK YⓤⒽ VⒺL
DⒾT ⒾS FⓄⓄR ⓄⓄ

PHRASEMAKER

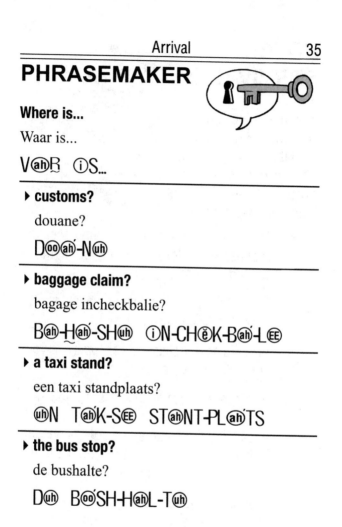

Where is...

Waar is...

V@hR ⓘS...

▶ **customs?**

douane?

D㏄@h´-N㎛

▶ **baggage claim?**

bagage incheckbalie?

B@h-H@h´-SH㎛ ⓘN-CH㊛K-B@h´-L㏍

▶ **a taxi stand?**

een taxi standplaats?

㎛N T@hK-S㏍ ST@hNT-PL@h´TS

▶ **the bus stop?**

de bushalte?

D㎛ B㏄´SH-H@hL-T㎛

HOTEL SURVIVAL

A wide selection of accommodations is available in major cities. The most complete range of facilities is found in five star hotels.

- Make reservations well in advance and request the address of the hotel to be written in Dutch.

- Do not leave valuables or cash in your room when you are not there!

- Be sure to purchase an adapter for your computer, music players, etc.

- It is a good idea to make sure you give your room number to persons you expect to call you. This can avoid confusion with Western names. Note that most budget hotels do not have phones in the room.

- It is also a good idea to bring your own alarm clock as you may be on your own for that important wake up call.

KEY WORDS

Hotel
Hotel

HO-TëL

Bellman
Hotelbediende

HO-TëL Bah-DEEN-Duh

Maid
Schoonmaakster

SHON-Mahk-STUr

Message
Bericht

Buh-RiKT

Reservation
Reservering

RA-SUr-FEER-uhN

Room service
Room service

ROOM SUr-ViS

Room
Kamer

Kah-MUr

CHECKING IN

My name is…

Mijn naam is...

MⒾN NⓐⓗM ⒾS...

I have a reservation.

Ik heb een reservering.

ⒾK HⒺⓑB ⓤⓗN BⒶ-SⓊⓡ-FⒺⒺⓑR-ⓤⓗN

Have you any vacancies?

Heeft u enige vrije kamers?

HⒶFT ⓄⓄ ⒶN-Hⓤⓗ
FBⒾ-Yⓤⓗ Kⓐⓗ-MⓊⓡS

What is the charge per night?

Hoeveel rekent u per nacht?

HⓄⓄ-FⒺⓑL BⒶ-KⓤⓗNT
ⓄⓄ PⒺⓑB NⓐⓗKT

My room key, please.

Mijn kamersleutel, alstublieft.

MⒾN Kⓐⓗ-MⓊⓡ-SLⓄⓄ-TⓤⓗL
ⓐⓗLS-TⓄⓄ-BLⒺⒺⓑFT

PHRASEMAKER

I would like a room with…

Ik wil graag een kamer met...

ⒾK VⒾL HⱤⓐH ⓊⒽN
Kⓐ-MⓊ MⒺT...

▸ **a bath**

een bad

ⓊⒽN BⓐⓗT

▸ **one bed**

een bed

ⓊⒽN BⒺT

▸ **two beds**

twee bedden

TVⒶ BⒺ-DⓊⒽN

▸ **a shower**

een douche

ⓊⒽN DⓄⓄSH

USEFUL PHRASES

My room key, please.

Mijn kamersleutel, alstublieft.

M(I)N K(ä)-M(Ur)-SL(oo)-T(uh)L
(ah)LS-T(oo)-BL(ee)FT

Are there any messages for me?

Zijn er enige berichten voor mij?

S(I)N (Ur) (A)N-H(uh)
B(ē)-R(ĕ)K-T(uh)N F(O)R M(I)

Where is the dining room?

Waar is de eetkamer?

V(ah)R (I)S D(uh) (A)T-K(ä)-M(Ur)

Are meals included?

Zijn de maaltijden inclusief?

S(I)N D(uh) M(ah)L-T(I)-D(uh)N
(I)N-KL(oo)-S(ee)F

What time is breakfast?

Hoe laat is er ontbijt?

H(oo) L(ah)T (I)S (ē)R (ou)NT-B(I)T

PHRASEMAKER
(WAKE UP CALL)

Please, wake me at...

Alstublieft, kunt u mij wakker maken om...

@LS-T@-BL@FT K@NT @ M①
V@K-@ M@-K@N ©M...

▸ **6:00** AM

zes uur 's morgens

S@S @B SM@B-H@NS

▸ **6:30** AM

half zeven 's morgens

H@F S@-F@ SM@B-H@NS

▸ **7:00** AM

zeven uur 's morgens

S@-F@N @B SM@B-H@NS

▸ **7:30** AM

half acht 's morgens

H@F @KTS SM@B-H@NS

▸ **8:00** AM

acht uur 's morgens

@KT @B SM@B-H@NS

PHRASEMAKER

I need…

Ik heb...

ⓘK Hⓔ︎B...

▸ **a babysitter**

een oppas nodig

ⓤN ⓞP-Pⓐ︎S Nⓞ-Dⓤ

▸ **a bellman**

een hotelbediende nodig

ⓤN Hⓞ-Tⓔ︎L Bⓐ-DⒺⒺN-Dⓤ Nⓞ-Dⓤ

▸ **more blankets**

meer dekens nodig

MⒶR DⒶ-Kⓤ︎NS Nⓞ-Dⓤ

▸ **a hotel safe**

een hotelkluis nodig

ⓤN Hⓞ-Tⓔ︎L-KLⓞ︎WS Nⓞ-Dⓤ

▸ **ice cubes**

ijsblokjes nodig

ⓘS-BLⓞK-Yⓤ︎S Nⓞ-Dⓤ

▶ **an extra key**

een extra sleutel nodig

(uh)N (e)K-STR(ah) SL(O)-T(uh)L N(O)-D(uh)

▶ **a maid**

een schoonmaakster nodig

(uh)N SCH(O)N-M(ah)K-ST(ur) N(O)-D(uh)

▶ **the manager**

de manager nodig

D(uh) M(a)-N(uh)-J(ur) N(O)-D(uh)

▶ **clean sheets**

nieuwe lakens nodig

N(EE)-V(uh) L(ah)-K(uh)NS N(O)-D(uh)

▶ **soap**

zeep nodig

S(a)P N(O)-D(uh)

▶ **toilet paper**

toiletpapier nodig

TW(ah)-L(e)T P(ah)-P(EE)R N(O)-D(uh)

▶ **more towels**

meer handdoeken nodig

M(EE)R H(ah)N-D(oo)-K(uh)N N(O)-D(uh)

PHRASEMAKER
(PROBLEMS)

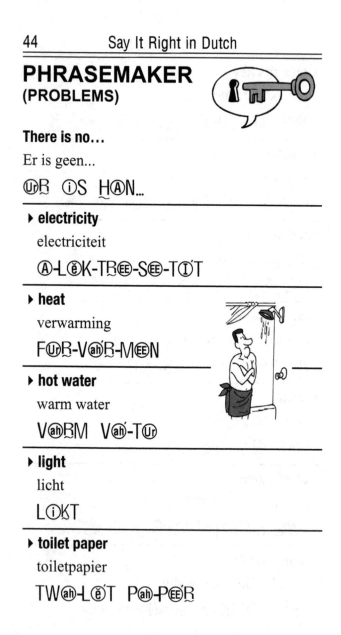

There is no…

Er is geen...

ⓊR ⒾS H🅐N...

▸ **electricity**

electriciteit

🅐-LⓔK-TRⒺⒺ-SⒺⒺ-TⒾT

▸ **heat**

verwarming

FⓊR-V🅐R-MⒺⒺN

▸ **hot water**

warm water

V🅐RM V🅐-TⓊr

▸ **light**

licht

LⒾKT

▸ **toilet paper**

toiletpapier

TW🅐-LⓔT P🅐-PⒺⒺR

PHRASEMAKER
(SPECIAL NEEDS)

Do you have…?

Heeft u...?

H◉FT ⓞⓞ...

▸ **an elevator?**

een lift?

◉N LⓘFT

▸ **a ramp?**

een ramp?

◉N Rⓐ◉MP

▸ **a wheelchair?**

een rolstoel?

◉N Rⓞ́L-STⓞⓞL

▸ **facilities for the disabled?**

gehandicapten faciliteiten?

Hⓤ-Hⓐ́N-Dⓔⓔ-Kⓐ́P-Tⓤ N
Fⓐ-Sⓘ-Lⓔⓔ-Tⓘ́-Tⓤ N

CHECKING OUT

The bill, please.

De rekening, alstublieft.

D⒰h R🅐-K⒰h-N🄴🄴N 🅐LS-T🅛-BL🄴🄴FT

There is a mistake!

Er is een misverstand!

⒰R ⒤S ⒰N M⒤S-F⒰r-ST🅐NT

Do you accept credit cards?

Accepteerd u creditkaarten?

🅐K-S🄴P-T🄴rT 🅛
KR🄴-D⒤T-K🅐R-T⒰N

Could you have my luggage brought down?

Kunt u mijn bagage laten brengen?

K⒰NT 🅛 M⒤N B🅐H-H🅐-SH⒰h
L🅐-T⒰N BR🄴N-H⒰N

Please call a taxi.

Alstublieft kunt u een taxi bellen.

@LS-T@-BL@FT K@NT @
@N T@K-S@ B@L-L@N

I had a very good time!

Ik heb een hele leuke tijd gehad!

@K H@B @N H@-L@
L@-K@ T@T H@-H@T

Thanks for everything.

Bedankt voor alles.

B@-D@NKT F@R @L-L@S

We'll see you next time.

We zien u de volgende keer.

V@ S@N @ D@
F@L-H@N-D@ K@R

Good-bye.

Tot ziens.

T@T S@NS

RESTAURANT SURVIVAL

Typical Dutch food is hearty and wholesome. The Dutch have always been internationally orientated and so you can expect to find cuisine from all over the world.

- Going Dutch is a slang term that means that each person eating at a restaurant or paying admission for entertainment pays for himself or herself, rather than one person paying for everyone. It is also called Dutch date and Dutch Treat.

- The Dutch have their own types of fast food. A Dutch fast-food meal often consists of a portion of french fries (called friet or patat) with mayonnaise.

- The Dutch have always been global explorers and so you can expect to find meals varying from Greece to the Orient and from China to Africa on Dutch dinner tables.

- Tipping at restaurants include 15% service and VAT. It is customary to leave small change when paying a bill.

KEY WORDS

Breakfast

Ontbijt

ÓNT-BⒾT

Lunch

Lunch

LⓄNCH

Dinner

Avond eten

ⓐĥ-VⓄⓄNT Ⓐ-TⓊĥN

Waiter

Ober

Ó-BⓊr

Waitress

Serveerster

SⓊr-FⒺⒺŔR-STⓊr

Restaurant

Restaurant

RⒺ̃S-TⓄⓌ-RⓐĥNT

USEFUL PHRASES

A table for...

Een tafel voor...

ⓤⒽN TⓐⒽ-FⓤⒽL FⓄⓇR...

2	4	6
twee	vier	zes
TVⒶ	FⒺⒺR	SⓔⒼS

The menu, please.

de menukaart, alstublieft.

DⓤⒽ MⓔⒼ-NⓄⓄ KⓐⒽRT
ⓐⒽLS-TⓄⓄ-BLⒺⒺFT

Separate checks, please.

Aparte rekeningen, alstublieft.

ⓐⒽ-PⓐⒽR-TⓤⒽ RⓐⒸ-KⓤⒽ-NⒺⒺN-ⓤⒽN
ⓐⒽLS-TⓄⓄ-BLⒺⒺFT

We are in a hurry.

We hebben een beetje haast.

VⓤⒽ HⓔⒼ-BⓤⒽN ⓤⒽN BⒶT-YⓤⒽ HⓐⒽST

What do you recommend?

Wat kunt u ons aanraden?

VⓐⒽT KⓄⓊNT ⓄⓄ ⓄⓃS ⓐⒽR-RⓐⒽ-DⓤⒽN

Please bring me...

Alstublieft breng mij....

@hLS-T@-BL@'FT BR@N M@...

Please bring us...

Alstublieft breng ons....

@hLS-T@-BL@'FT BR@N @NS...

I'm hungry.

Ik heb honger.

@K H@B H@N-H@r

I'm thirsty.

Ik heb dorst.

@K H@B D@RST

Is service included?

Is fooi geven inclusief betalen?

@S F@y H@'F@N
@N-KL@'-S@F B@-T@'-L@N ?

The bill, please.

De rekening, alstublieft.

D@ R@'-K@-N@N @hLS-T@-BL@'FT

POPULAR DUTCH MEALS

- A **Dutch breakfast** usually consists of fresh bread, cheese, cooked meats and sausage, butter and hagelslag (chocolate sprinkles), jam or honey, and often a boiled egg.

- **Broodjes** (sandwiches) are a common lunch or daytime snack.

- **Dinner**, traditionally served early by international standards, starts at about 6 o'clock in the evening.

- **Poffertjes** (pancakes) served with butter and sugar are a teatime favorite.

- **Patat** or french fries is a very common snack and is usually served with mayonnaise or other sometimes exotics dips. There are usually small establishments all over major cities devoted exclusively to selling french fries and the quality is exceptional.

- **Desserts** often include vla (milk pudding) or yogurt. Regional variants include bread pudding made from old bread, milk, butter, and sugar.

NATIONAL DRINKS

- Coffee, tea, chocolate, and fruit juice are drunk at breakfast.

- The local spirit is Dutch gin, called Jenever, which is normally taken straight and chilled as a chaser with a glass of beer. It is sometimes drunk with mixers and is available in numerous flavors.

- The most popular beer brands in Amsterdam are Amstel and Heineken.

- Legal drinking age is 16 to drink beer and wine and 18 to drink spirits

COFFEE SHOPS

- Amsterdam has around 150 coffee shops, which operate for the sole purpose of selling marijuana and hashish and letting people smoke it right there.

BEVERAGE LIST

Coffee
Koffie

KO-FEE

Decaffeinated coffee
Cafeinevrije koffie

Kah-Fah-EE-Nah-FRI-Yuh KO-FEE

Tea
Thee

TA

Cream
Koffiemelk

KO-FEE-MELK

Sugar
Suiker

SOW-KUr

Lemon
Citroen

SEE-TROON

Milk

Melk

MⓔLK

Hot chocolate

Warme chocomelk

VⓐR-MⓊⒽ SHⓄ-KⓄ-MⓔLK

Juice

Sap

SⓐP

Orange juice

Sinaasappelsap

SⓄN-ⓐ-Sⓐ-PⓄⓄL SⓐP

Ice water

Ijswater

ⓘS-Vⓐ-TⓊⓡ

Bottle water

Spa blauw

SPⓐ BLⓄⓦ

Ice

Ijsblokjes

ⓘS-BLⓄK-YⓊⒽS

AT THE BAR

Bartender

Ober

Ō-BŪr

Cocktail

Cocktail

KŌK-TĀL

With ice

Met ijsblokjes

MĕT   ĪS-BLŌK-YuhS

Without ice

Zonder ijs

SŌN-DŪr   ĪS

With lemon

Met citroen

MĕT   SEE-TRooN

PHRASEMAKER

I would like a glass of...

Ik zou graag een glas...

ⓘK Sⓞ HⒷⓐⓗH ⓤⓗN HLⓐⓗS...

▸ **champagne**

champagne willen hebben

SHⓐⓗM-PⓐⓗN-Yⓐⓗ VⓞⓘL-LⓤⓗN Hⓔ̈-BⓤⓗN

▸ **beer**

bier willen hebben

BⒺⒺR VⓞⓘL-LⓤⓗN Hⓔ̈-BⓤⓗN

▸ **wine**

wijn willen hebben

VⓘN VⓞⓘL-LⓤⓗN Hⓔ̈-BⓤⓗN

▸ **red wine**

rode wijn willen hebben

Rⓞ-Dⓤⓗ VⓘN VⓞⓘL-LⓤⓗN Hⓔ̈-BⓤⓗN

▸ **white wine**

witte wijn willen hebben

Vⓘ-Tⓤⓗ VⓘN VⓞⓘL-LⓤⓗN Hⓔ̈-BⓤⓗN

FAMILIAR FOODS

On the following pages you will
find lists of foods you are familiar
with, along with other information
such as basic utensils and preparation
instructions.

A polite way to get a waiter's or waitress's attention is
to say **"Mag ik u vragen om?"**, which means, **"May
I ask?"**, followed by your request and thank you.

May I ask?

Mag ik u vragen om...?

M@H ⓘK ⓞⓞ FR@-HⓤN ⓞM...

Please bring me...

Alstublieft brengt u mij...

@LS-Tⓞⓞ-BLⒺⒺ'FT BR@NT ⓞⓞ Mⓘ...

Thank you.

Dank u wel.

D@NK ⓞⓞ VⒺL

STARTERS

Appetizers
Voorafje

FOOR-ah-F-Yuh

Bread and butter
Brood en boter

BROT eN BO-Tur

Cheese
Kaas

Kah-S

Fruit
Fruit

FRow-T

Salad
Salade

Sah-L-ah-Duh

Soup
Soep

SooP

MEATS

Bacon

Spek

SP(e)K

Beef

Vlees

FL(a)S

Beef steak

Biefstuk

B(ee)F-ST(ou)K

Ham

Ham

H(ah)M

Lamb

Lamsvlees

L(ah)MS-FL(a)S

Pork

Varkensvlees

F(ah)R-K(uh)NS-FL(a)S

Veal

Kalfsvlees

K(ah)FS-FL(a)S

POULTRY

Baked chicken

Gebakken kip

H̲ᵁʰ-BᵃʰK-KᵁʰN KⁱP

Grilled chicken

Gegrilde kip

H̲ᵁʰ-HRⁱL-Dᵁʰ KⁱP

Fried chicken

Gefrituurde kip

H̲ᵁʰ-FRᴱᴱ-Tᵒᵒʀ-Dᵁʰ KⁱP

Duck

Eend

ᴬNT

Goose

Gans

H̲ᵃʰNS

Turkey

Kalkoen

KᵃʰL-KᵒᵒʹN

SEAFOOD

Fish

Vis

FⓘS

Lobster

Kreeft

KⓇⒶFT

Oysters

Oesters

⓪⓪S-TⓊ⒭S

Salmon

Zalm

SⓐⓗLM

Shrimp

Garnalen

HⓐⓗⓇ-Nⓐⓗ-LⓊⓗN

Tuna

Tonijn

T⓪-NⓘⓘN

OTHER ENTREES

Sandwich
Broodje

BRŌD-Yᵘʰ

Hot dog
Hot dog

HOT DᵃʰG

Hamburger
Hamburger

HᵃʰM-BᵁʳHᵁʳ

French fries
Franse frietjes

FRᵃʰN-Sᵘʰ FRᴱᴱT-Yᵉˢ

Pasta
Pasta

PᵃʰS-Tᵃʰ

Pizza
Pizza

PᴱᴱT-Sᵃʰ

VEGETABLES

Carrots

Wortels

VOR-Tuh LZ

Corn

Mais

MIS

Mushrooms

Champignon

SHahM-PEE-YON

Onions

Uien

ow-YuhN

Potato

Aardappel

ahBT-ahP-PuhL

Rice

Rijst

BIST

Tomato

Tomaat

TO-Mah T

FRUITS

Apple

Appel

@P-PⓊL

Banana

Banaan

B@-N@N

Grapes

Druiven

DRⒾ-FⓊN

Lemon

Citroen

SⒺ-TRⓄⓄN

Orange

Sinaasappel

SⒺ-N@-S@-PⓊL

Strawberry

Aardbeien

@RT-BⒾ-ⓊN

Watermelon

Watermeloen

V@-TⓊⲢ-MⓊ-LⓄⓄN

DESSERT

Desserts

Nagerecht

N@-H@-R@KT

Apple pie

Appeltaart

@P-P@L-T@RT

Cherry pie

Kersentaart

K@-S@N-T@RT

Pastries

Gebakjes

H@-B@K-Y@S

Candy

Snoepjes

SN@P-Y@S

Ice cream

Ijs

ⒾS

Ice cream cone

Ijshoorn

ⒾS-HⓄ-RⓤⓗN

Chocolate

Chocolade

SHⓄ-KⓄ-Lⓐⓗ-Dⓤⓗ

Strawberry

Aardbeien

ⓐⓗRT-BⒾ-ⓔN

Vanilla

Vanille

Fⓐⓗ-NⒺⒺL-Yⓤⓗ

CONDIMENTS

Butter

Boter

BO-TUr

Ketchup

Ketchup

KëT-CHuhP

Mayonnaise

Mayonaise

MI-O-Në-Zuh

Mustard

Mosterd

MOS-TUrT

Salt

Zout

ZowT

Pepper

Peper

PA-PUr

Sugar

Suiker

Sow-KUr

SETTINGS

A cup

Een kopje

uhN KOP-Yuh

A glass

Een glas

uhN HLahS

A spoon

Een lepel

uhN LA-POL

A fork

Een vork

uhN FORK

A knife

Een mes

uhN MeS

A plate

Een bord

uhN BORT

A napkin

Een servet

uhN SUr-FeT

HOW DO YOU WANT IT COOKED?

Baked

Gebakken

H͟uh-Bah´K-Kuh N

Grilled

Gegrild

H͟uh-H͟Rͦ́LT

Steamed

Gestoomd

H͟uh-STͦMT

Fried

Gebakken

H͟uh-Bah´K-KuhN

Medium

Medium

Mͤͤ´-Dͤͤ-uhM

Well done

Doorgebakken

Dͦ́R-H͟uh-Bah K-KuhN

PROBLEMS

I didn't order this.

Ik heb dit niet besteld.

ⒾK HⓔB DⒾT NⒺⒺT BⓔS-Tⓔ'LT

Please check the bill.

Kunt u deze rekening controleren?

KⓤⓄNT ⓄⓄ DⒶ'-Sⓤⓗ RⒶ-Kⓤⓗ-NⒺⒺN
KⓄN-TRⓄ-Lⓔ'-RⓤⓗN ?

PRAISE

Very good!

Heel goed!

HⒶL HⓄⓄT

GETTING AROUND

Getting around in a foreign country can be an adventure in itself! Taxi and bus drivers do not always speak English, so it is essential to be able to give simple directions. The words and phrases in this chapter will help you get where you're going.

- Trams and buses run from about 6 am to midnight daily.

- Every day, almost one million people travel by tram, bus, or metro in Amsterdam.

- The most frequently used trams by visitors are the 1, 2, and 5, which stop at the central Dam Square and, along with 6, 7, and 10, also stop at Leidseplein square.

- Bicycles are everywhere in Holland so be careful while driving and walking. In big cities like Amsterdam, the dance between autos, pedestrians, bicycles, motorcycles, and motor scooters is amazing!! It is organized chaos!

- There are several bicycle rental companies in most major cities but be prepared to pay a substantial deposit.

- Amsterdam is considered the bicycle capital of the world.

KEY WORDS

Airport

Vliegveld

FL(EE)H̰-F(ŏ)LT

Bus Stop

Bushalte

B(oo)'SH-H(ah)L-T(uh)

Car Rental Agency

Auto Verhuur

(ow)'-T(ŏ) F(ĕ)R-H(oo)'R

Taxi Stand

Taxi Standplaats

T(ah)K-S(EE) ST(ah)'NT-PL(ah)TS

Train Station

Trein Station

TR(Ī)N ST(ah)'T-SH(ŏ)N

AIR TRAVEL

Airport
Vliegveld

FL(EE)H̃-F(ē)LT

A one-way ticket, please
Een enkele reis, alstublieft

(ē)N (ē)N-K(uh)-L(uh) R(I)S
(ah)LS-T(oo)-BL(EE)FT

A round-trip ticket
Een retour ticket

(uh)N R(uh)-T(oo)R T(i)-K(ē)T

First class
Eerste klas

(EE)R-ST(uh) KL(ah)S

How much do I owe?
Hoeveel ben ik u schuldig?

H(o)-F(a)L B(uh)N (I)K (oo) SH(uh)L-D(uh)

The gate
De gate / tunnel

D(uh) G(a)T / T(uh)-N(ē)L

PHRASEMAKER

I would like a seat...

Ik wil graag een stoel...

ⓘK VⓘL HⓇⓐ̰Ḫ ⓤⓗN STⓞL...

▸ **in first class**

in de eerste klas

ⓘN Dⓤⓗ Ⓔ̲Ⓡ-STⓤⓗ KLⓐS

▸ **next to the window**

naast het raam

NⓐⓗST HⓔⓉ ⓇⓐⓗM

▸ **on the aisle**

aan het binnenpad

ⓐⓗN Hⓔ̄T Bⓘ́N-Nⓔⓝ-PⓐⓗT

▸ **near the exit**

naast de uitgang

NⓐⓗST Dⓤⓗ ⓞⓦT-Hⓐ̰ⓗN

BY BUS

Bus

Bus

B@S

Where is the bus stop?

Waar is de bushalte?

V@R @S D@ B@SH-H@L-T@

Do you go to...?

Gaat u naar...?

H@T @ N@R...

What is the fare?

Hoeveel kost het?

H@-F@L K@ST H@T

Do I need exact change?

Heb ik contant geld nodig?

H@B @K K@N-T@NT
H@LT N@-D@

PHRASEMAKER

Which bus goes to...

Welke bus gaat naar...

VĔL-Kᵘʰ BᵒᵘS HᵃʰT NᵃʰR...

▸ **the beach?**

het strand?

HĔT STRᵃʰNT

▸ **the market?**

de markt?

Dᵘʰ MᵃʰRKT

▸ **the airport?**

het vliegveld?

HĔT FLᵉᵉH-FĔLT

▸ **the train station?**

het trein station?

HĔT TRⓄN STᵃʰT-SHⓄN

BY CAR

Can you help me?

Kunt u mij helpen?

K⒪NT ⓞⓞ M① H⒠L-P⒰N

My car won't start.

Mijn auto start niet.

M①N ⒲-T⒪ ST⒜RT N⒠T

Can you fix it?

Kunt u het maken?

K⒪NT ⓞⓞ H⒠T M⒜-K⒰N

What will it cost?

Wat gaat het kosten?

V⒜T H⒜T H⒠T K⒪S-T⒰N

How long will it take?

Hoe lang gaat het duren?

H⒪ L⒜N H⒜T H⒠T D⒪⒪-R⒰N

PHRASEMAKER

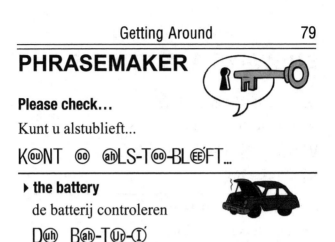

Please check…

Kunt u alstublieft...

KⓊNT ⓄⓄ ⓐⓗLS-TⓄⓄ-BLⒺⒺFT...

▸ **the battery**

de batterij controleren

DⓊⓗ Bⓐⓗ-TⓊr-Ⓘ
KⓄN-TRⓄ-LⒺⒺ-RⓔN

▸ **the brakes**

de remmen controleren

DⓊⓗ RⓔM-MⓊⓗN
KⓄN-TRⓄ-LⒺⒺ-RⓔN

▸ **the oil**

de olie controleren

DⓊⓗ Ⓞ-LⒺⒺ KⓄN-TRⓄ-LⒺⒺ-RⓔN

▸ **the tires**

de banden controleren

DⓊⓗ BⓐⓗN-DⓊⓗN KⓄN-TRⓄ-LⒺⒺ-RⓔN

▸ **the water**

het water controleren

HⓔT Vⓐⓗ-TⓊr KⓄN-TRⓄ-LⒺⒺ-RⓔN

SUBWAYS AND TRAINS

Where is the train station?

Waar is het trein station?

V@B ⒤S H@T TR@N
ST@T-SH@N

A one-way ticket, please.

Een enkele reis, alstublieft.

@N @N-K@-L@ R⒤S
@LS-T@-BL@FT

A round-trip ticket.

Een retour ticket alstublieft.

@N R@-T@R T⒤-K@T
@LS-T@-BL@FT

First class

Eerste klas

@B-ST@ KL@S

Second class

Tweede klas

TV@-D@ KL@S

What is the fare?

Wat is de prijs?

V@hT ⓘS D@h PR̃ⓘS

Is this seat taken?

Is deze stoel bezet?

ⓘS D@̃-S@h
STⓄL B@h-S@̃T

Do I have to change trains?

Moet ik overstappen?

MⓄT ⓘK Ⓞ́-F@r-ST@h-P@hN

Where are we?

Waar zijn we?

V@hR SⓘN V@h

BY TAXI

Please call a taxi for me.

Kunt u alstublieft een taxi bellen voor mij?

K⒪NT ⒨ ⒜LS-T⒨-BL⒠FT
B⒠L-L⒰N F⒪R M⒤

Are you available?

Bent u beschikbaar?

B⒠NT ⒨ B⒰-SH⒤K-B⒜R ?

I want to go.

Ik wil gaan.

⒤K V⒤L H⒜N
      ~

Stop here, please.

Kunt u hier stoppen, alstublieft?

K⒪NT ⒨ H⒠R ST⒪P-P⒰N
⒜LS-T⒨-BL⒠FT

Please wait.

Alstublieft kunt u wachten.

⒜LS-T⒨-BL⒠FT K⒪NT ⒨ V⒜K-T⒰N

How much do I owe?

Hoeveel krijgt u van mij?

H⒪-F⒜L KR⒤KT ⒨ F⒜N M⒤

PHRASEMAKER

The simplest way to get to
where you want to go is to
name the destination and simply say, **"please**."

▸ **This address...**

Dit adres....

DⓘT ⓐh-DRⓔ́S...

Have someone at your hotel write down the address
for you in Dutch.

▸ **This hotel**...

Dit hotel...

DⓘT HⓄ-TⓔL...

▸ **Airport...**

Het vliegveld....

HⓔT FLⓔⒺH-FⓔLT...

▸ **Subway station...**

Het metrostation...

HⓔT MⒶ́-TRⓄ-STⓐhT-SⒺⒺⓄN...

...please.

...alstublieft.

...ⓐhLS-Tⓞⓞ-BLⒺⒺ́FT

SHOPPING

Whether you plan a major shopping spree or just need to purchase some basic necessities, the following information is useful.

- Shopping hours: In general shops are open from Tuesday thru Saturday from 9 AM to 5 PM. Most open late on Monday morning and many open on Sunday with shorter hours.

- Credit/debit cards and ATMs: American Express, Diners Club, MasterCard, and Visa are accepted. ATMs are widely available. Keep in mind that you will be asked how many euros you would like to withdraw, and you must make the calculation as to how much you are actually taking out in dollars.

- There are many local markets in towns throughout the Netherlands and they are well worth seeking out. From flower markets to clothes markets and even food markets it is a great opportunity to mingle with the locals and find great deals. Some are open daily and some only on the weekend but they are always easy to find.

KEY WORDS

Credit card

Creditcard

KR█-D█T K█RT

Money

Geld

H█LT

Euro

Euro

Y█-R█

Sale

Verkopen

F█R-K█-P█N

Store

Winkel

V█N-K█L

Traveler's checks

Reis cheque

R█S SH█K

USEFUL PHRASES

Can you help me?

Kunt u me helpen?

K⓪NT ⓪⓪ M⓾ H⑧L-P⓾N

I'm just looking.

Ik kijk alleen.

①K K①K ⓐL-LⓐN

How much?

Hoeveel kost het?

H①-FⓐL K①ST H⑧T

No, thank you.

Nee, bedankt.

Nⓐ B⓾-DⓐNKT

Is it very expensive?

Is het heel erg duur?

①S H⑧T HⓐL ⑧RH D⓪⓪R

That's too expensive.

Dat is te duur.

DⓐT ①S T⓾ D⑩R

Can't you give me a discount?

Kan ik wat korting krijgen?

K@N ⓘK V@T K◎R-T@N
KR̲ⓘ-H̲uhN

I'll take it.

Ik neem het.

ⓘK N@M H@T

A receipt please.

Een kwitantie, alstublieft.

uhN KV@-T@NT-S@ @LS-T◎-BL@FT

Can you wrap it?

Kunt u het inpakken?

K◎NT ⊚ H@T ⓘN-P@K-K uhN

Can you ship it?

Kunt u het versturen?

K◎NT ⊚ H@T F@r-ST◎-R uhN

Thats all thanks.

Meer niet dank u.

M@R N@T D@NK ⊚

SHOPS AND SERVICES

Bakery

Bakker

B@K-K@r

Bank	**Hair salon / Barbershop**
Bank	Kapper
B@NK	K@P-P@r

Jewelry store

Juwelier

Y@-V@h-L@R

Bookstore

Boekenwinkel

B@-K@hN-V@N-K@hL

News stand

Krantenwinkel

KR@N-T@hN-V@N-K@hL

Camera shop

Foto winkel

F@-T@   V@N-K@hL

Pharmacy

Apotheek

@h-P@-T@K

SHOPPING LIST

On the following pages, you will find some common items you may need to purchase on your trip.

Aspirin

Aspirine

@S-P㉺-R㉺-N㉾

Cigarettes

Sigaretten

S㉺-H@-R㊝-T㊝N

Deodorant

Deodorant

D@-O-DO-R@NT

Dress

Jurk

Y㊍RK

Film (camera)

Film

F㋛LM

Perfume

Parfum

P@B-F@M

Razor blades

Scheer mesjes

SH@B M@S-Y@S

Shampoo

Shampoo

SH@M-P©

Shaving cream

Scheerschuim

SH@B-SH©M

Shirt

Shirt

SH@BT

Sunglasses

Zonnebrilen

Z©N-N@-BB©-L@N

Suntan oil

Zonnebrand

ZON-Nuh-BRauNT

Toothbrushes

Tandenborstel

TahN-DuhN-BOB-STuhL

Toothpaste

Tandpasta

TahNT-PahS-Tah

Water

Water

Vah-TUr

Water (mineral)

Water mineraal

Vah-TUr MEE-NUr-ahL

ESSENTIAL SERVICES

THE BANK

As a traveler in a foreign country, your primary contact with banks will be to exchange money.

- The official Dutch currency is the euro, divided into cents.

- Banks are usually open from Mondays to Fridays between 9:30 AM. and 5:30 PM.

- Currency can be changed at banks, currency exchange booths, and hotels.

- ATM's are widely available in major cities. Check with your bank to see if your card is accepted and get exact locations.

- Cash advances on credit cards can be handled at the bank but may be subject to a higher commission.

- ATMs offer good exchange rates although there may be some hidden fees.

- Remember that what you get in euros is different from what you are actually taking out in dollars so you must stay abreast of the exchange rates.

KEY WORDS

Bank

Bank

B@NK

Exchange bureau

Wisselkantoor

VⓘS-SⓤhL-K@N-TⓄB

Money

Geld

HⓔLT

Money order

Geld order

HⓔLT ⓄB-Dⓤr

ATM

Geldautomaat

HⓔLT-ⓄW-TⓄ-M@T

Euro

Euro

Yⓞⓞ-BⓄ

USEFUL PHRASES

Where is the bank?
Waar is de bank?

V(ah)R (i)S D(uh) B(ah)NK

What time does the bank open?
Hoe laat gaat de bank open?

H(o) L(ah)T H̃(ah)T D(uh)
B(ah)NK (o)-P(uh)N

Where is the exchange office?
Waar is het wisselkantoor?

V(ah)R (i)S H(e)T
V(i)S-S(uh)L-K(ah)N-T(o)R

What time does the exchange office open?
Hoe laat gaat het wisselkantoor open?

H(o) L(ah)T H̃(ah)T H(e)T
V(i)S-S(uh)L-K(ah)N-T(o)R (o)-P(uh)N

Can I change dollars here?
Kan ik hier mijn dollars wisselen?

K(ah)N (i)K H(ee)R M(i)N
D(o)-L(ah)RS V(i)-S(uh)-L(uh)N

What is the exchange rate?

Wat is de wisselkoers?

V@T ⓘS D@ VⓘS-S@L-K@RS

I would like large bills.

Ik zou graag grote biljetten willen hebben.

ⓘK Z@ HR@H
HR@-T@ BⓘL-Y@T-@N
VⓘL-L@N H@B-B@N

I would like small bills.

Ik zou graag kleine biljetten willen hebben.

ⓘK Z@ HR@H
KLⓘ-N@ BⓘL-Y@T-@N
VⓘL-L@N H@B-B@N

I need change.

Ik heb wisselgeld nodig.

ⓘK H@B
VⓘS-S@L-H@LT N@-D@

Do you have an ATM?

Heeft u een geldautomaat?

H@FT ⓞⓞ @N
H@LT-@W-T@-M@T

POST OFFICE

If you are planning on sending
letters and postcards, be sure
to send them early so that you
don't arrive home before they do.

KEY WORDS

Air mail

Lucht post

LⓊKT PⓄST

Letter

Brief

BRⒺⒺF

Post office

Postkantoor

PⓄST-KⓐN-TⓄⒷ

Postcard

Briefkaart

BRⒺⒺF-KⓐⒷT

Stamp

Postzegel

PⓄST-ZⒶ-HⓊL

USEFUL PHRASES

Where is the post office?

Waar is het postkantoor?

VⓐⓇ ⒾS HⓔT PⓄ'ST-KⓐN-TⓄⓇ

What time does the post office open?

Hoe laat gaat het postkantoor open?

HⓄ LⓐT HⓐT HⓔT
PⓄ'ST-KⓐN-TⓄⓇ Ⓞ'-PⓊN

I need...

Ik heb ... nodig

ⒾK HⓔB......NⓄ'-Dⓤ

I need stamps.

Ik heb postzegels nodig.

ⒾK HⓔB PⓄ'ST-ZⒶ-HⓊLS NⓄ'-Dⓤ

I need an envelope.

Ik heb een envelope nodig.

ⒾK HⓔB ⓊN ⓐN-FⓊ-LⓄ'P NⓄ'-Dⓤ

I need a pen.

Ik heb een pen nodig.

ⒾK HⓔB ⓊN PⓔN NⓄ'-Dⓤ

TELEPHONE

Placing phone calls in Holland is easy! Make sure you have euro coins with you.

- You can still find pay phones in the cities of the Netherlands but be sure you have euro coins.

- Internet cafes seem to be everywhere and are incredibly convenient. You can go on the internet and are timed and then you simply pay the clerk. Long distance calls are handled in the same manner.

- The police, fire, and ambulance emergency telephone number is 112.

- Dial 00 + 1+ area code + phone number to call the U.S. or Canada from the Netherlands or Belgium.

- Dial 00 + 44 + area code (minus the first 0) + phone number to call the U.K.

KEY WORDS

Information

Informatie

ⓘN-FⓄB-Mⓐ͞h-Tㄸ

Long distance call

Lange afstand bellen

Lⓐ͞h-Gⓤh   ⓐ͞hF-STⓐhNT   BㄸͭL-LⓤhN

Operator

Operator

Ⓞ́-PⓊr-Ⓐ-TⓊr

Phone book

Telefoonboek

Tㄸ-Lⓤh-FⓄ́N-BⓞⓞK

Public telephone

Publieke telefoon

Pⓞⓞ-BLㄸ́-Kⓤh   Tㄸ-Lⓤh-FⓄ́N

Telephone

Telefoon

Tㄸ-Lⓤh-FⓄ́N

USEFUL PHRASES

Where is the telephone?

Waar is de telefoon?

V(ah)R (i)S D(uh) T(e)-L(uh)-FO'N

Where is the public telephone?

Waar is de publieke telefoon?

V(ah)R (i)S D(uh)
P(oo)-BL(EE)'-K(uh) T(e)-L(uh)-FO'N

May I use your telephone?

Mag ik uw telefoon gebruiken?

M(ah)K (i)K (oo) T(e)-L(uh)-FO'N
H(uh)-BR(ow)'-K(uh)N

Operator, I don't speak Dutch.

Mevrouw, meneer ik spreek geen nederlands.

M(uh)-FR(ow)' M(uh)-N(EE)'R
(i)K SPR(a)K
H(a)N N(a)'-D(ur)-L(ah)NTS

I want to call this number...

Ik zou graag dit nummer willen bellen...

ⒾK ZⓄⓌ HⓇⓐhH DⒾT Nⓞⓞ-MⓊr
VⒾL-LⓊhN BⒺL-LⓊhN...

1 een ⒶN	2 twee TVⒶ	3 drie DRⒺⒺ
4 vier FⒺⒺR	5 vijf FⒾF	6 zes ZⒺS
7 zeven ZⒶ-FⓊhN	8 acht ⓐhKT	9 negen NⒶ-HⓊhN
*	0 nul NⓞⓞL	#

SIGHTSEEING AND ENTERTAINMENT

The correct name of the country is Netherlands and the word Holland is actually just a reference to the western section of the country.

- **Tulips:** Every year millions of tourists visit Keukenhof, a showpiece of flower beds near the small town of Lisse. Keukenhof is about an hour out of Amsterdam by car, bus or train and is open from 8 AM to 7.30 PM.

- **Rembrandt Museum:** The house where Rembrandt lived between 1639 and 1658 is now a museum. Today the Rembrandt House Museum attracts a great many visitors with its permanent display of Rembrandt's etchings and important exhibitions.

- **Amsterdam:** The capital and largest city of the Netherlands. Amsterdam's main attractions, include its historic canals, the Rijksmuseum, the Van Gogh Museum, Anne Frank House and of course its world famous red-light district.

KEY WORDS

Admission

Entreegeld

ⓤN-TRⒶ-HⒺLT

Map

Kaart

KⒶRT

Reservation

Reservering

RⒶ-SⒺR-FⒺR-ⒺN

Ticket

Ticket / kaartje

TⒾ-KⒺT / KⒶRT-Yⓤ

Tour

Rondreis

RⓄNT-RⒾS

Tour guide

Reis gids

RⒾS HⒾTS

USEFUL PHRASES

Where is the tourist agency?

Waar is het toeristenkantoor?

VahR IS HёT
Too-REE-STёN-KahN-TOR

Where do I buy a ticket?

Waar kan ik een ticket kopen?

VahR KahN IK uhN
TI-KёT KO-PuhN

How much?

Hoeveel?

Hoo-FEEL

How long?

Hoe lang?

Hoo LahNH

When?

Wanneer?

VahN-NEER

Where?

Waar?

VahR

Do I need reservations?

Moet ik reserveren?

M⊙⊙T ⓘK Rⓐ-Sⓤr-FⓔⓔR-ⓤⓗN

Does the guide speak English?

Spreekt de gids engels?

SPRⓐⓀT Dⓤⓗ
Hⓘ̱TS ⓔ̱N-HⓤⓗLS

How much do children pay?

Hoeveel moeten kinderen betalen?

H⊙⊙-Fⓐ́L M⊙⊙-TⓤⓗN
Kⓘ́N-Dⓤⓗ-RⓤⓗN Bⓔ̱-Tⓐⓗ́-LⓤⓗN

I need your help.

Ik heb je help nodig.

ⓘK Hⓔ̱B Yⓤⓗ Hⓔ̱LP N⊙-Dⓤⓗ́

Thank you.

Bedankt.

Bⓤⓗ-Dⓐⓗ́NKT

PHRASEMAKER

May I invite you to…

Mag ik je uitnodigen om naar...

M@H ⓘK Y⑩

⑩T-N⓪-Tⓘ-H⑩N ⓄM N@B...

▶ **a concert?**

een concert te gaan?

⑩N KⓄN-S⑪T T⑩ H@N

▶ **to dance?**

een dansfees te gaan?

⑩N D@NS-F⑯ST T⑩ H@N

▶ **to dinner?**

te gaan eten?

T⑩ H@N Ⓐ-T⑩N

▶ **to the movies?**

de film te gaan?

D⑩ FⓘLM T⑩

▶ **the theater?**

het theater te gaan?

H⑯T TⒶ-ah-T⑪ T⑩ H@N

PHRASEMAKER

Where can I find...

Waar kan ik...

V@B K@N ⓘK...

▸ **a health club?**

een gezondheidsclub vinden?

⓵N Hⓤ-SⓄNT-HⓘTS-KLⓄB VⓘN-Dⓤ N

▸ **a swimming pool?**

een zwembad vinden?

⓵N SVⓔM-B@D VⓘN-Dⓤ N

▸ **a tennis court?**

een tennisbaan vinden?

⓵N TⓔN-NⓘS-B@N VⓘN-Dⓤ N

▸ **a golf course?**

een golfbaan vinden?

⓵N GⓄLF-B@N VⓘN-Dⓤ N

HEALTH

Hopefully you will not need medical attention on your trip. If you do, it is important to communicate basic information regarding your condition.

- Travelers to Holland are urged to obtain overseas medical insurance, which includes hospitalization and medical evacuation.

- If you take prescription medicine, carry your prescription with you.

- Take a small first-aid kit with you. You may want to include basic cold, anti-diarrhea, and allergy medications. However, you should be able to find most items like aspirin locally.

- Holland has state of the art medical facilities so that is not an issue.

- Hint: The easiest way to find a doctor is to find a pharmacy first. They generally keep a list of nearby physicians who cater to tourists.

KEY WORDS

Ambulance
Ambulance

ⓐM-Bⓞⓞ-Lⓐⓝ-TSⓤⓗ

Dentist
Tandarts

TⓐⓝT-ⓐⓗRTS

Doctor
Dokter

DⓞⓀ-TⓊr

Emergency
Noodgeval

NⓞⓉ-Hⓤⓗ-FⓐⓗL

Hospital
Ziekenhuis

Zⓔⓔ-KⓤⓗN-HⓞⓦS

Prescription
Recept uitschrijven

Rⓔ-SⓔⓟT ⓞⓦT-SHRⓘ-FⓤⓗN

USEFUL PHRASES

I am sick.

Ik ben ziek.

ⒾK BⒺN ZⒾK

I need a doctor.

Ik heb een dokter nodig.

ⒾK HⒺB ⓊⱧN

DOK-TⓊr NOO-DⓊⱧ

It's an emergency!

Het is een noodgeval!

HⒺT ⒾS ⓊⱧN

NOOT-HⓊⱧ-FⓐⱧL

Call an ambulance!

Bel een ambulance!

BⒺL ⓊⱧN ⓐⱧM-BⓄⓄ-LⓐⱧNT-SⓊⱧ

I'm allergic to...

Ik ben allergisch voor...

ⒾK BⒺN ⓐL-LⓊ́-ⒽⒾSH FⓄR...

I'm pregnant.

Ik ben in verwachting.

ⒾK BⒺN ⒾN FⒺR-VⓐⓀ-TⒺN

I'm diabetic.

Ik ben diabetisch.

ⒾK BⒺN DⒺⓐ-BⒶ́-TⒾSH

I have a heart condition.

Ik heb hartproblemen.

ⒾK HⒺB HⓐRT-PRⓄ-BLⒶ́-MⓊN

I have high blood pressure.

Ik heb een hoge bloeddruk.

ⒾK HⒺB ⓊN
HⓄ́-HⓊ BLⓄⓄD-RⓄⓊK

I have low blood pressure.

Ik heb een lage bloeddruk.

ⒾK HⒺB ⓊN
Lⓐ́-HⓊ BLⓄⓄD-RⓄⓊK

PHRASEMAKER

I need...

Ik heb...

ⒾK HⒺB...

▶ **a doctor**

een dokter nodig

ⓊⒽN DⓄK-TⓊr NⓄ-DⓊⒽ

▶ **a dentist**

een tandarts nodig

ⓊⒽN TⓐⒽN-DⓐⒽRTS NⓄ-DⓊⒽ

▶ **a nurse**

een zuster nodig

ⓊⒽN ZⓄⓄS-TⓊr NⓄ-DⓊⒽ

▶ **an optician**

een opticien nodig

ⓊⒽN ⓄP-TⒺⒺ-SHⒺN NⓄ-DⓊⒽ

▶ **a pharmacy**

een apotheker nodig

ⓊⒽN ⓐⒽ-PⓄ-TⓐⒾKⓊr NⓄ-DⓊⒽ

PHRASEMAKER
(AT THE PHARMACY)

Do you have…

Heb je voor mij…

HĕB Yuh FOⓇ M① …

▶ **aspirin?**

een aspirine?

uhN ahS-PEE-REE-Nuh

▶ **Band-Aids?**

verbandtrommel?

FUr-BahNT-RO-Muhl

▶ **cough syrup?**

hoestsiroop?

HOST-S①-ROP

▶ **ear drops?**

oordruppels?

OR-DRou-Puhls

▶ **eye drops?**

oogdruppels?

OH-DRouP-Puhls

BUSINESS TRAVEL

It is important to show appreciation and interest in another person's language and culture, particularly when doing business. A few well-pronounced phrases can make a great impression.

- Business dealings can be very bureaucratic. There are many procedures and a great deal of paperwork.

- The Dutch often engage in long, critical discussions before reaching a decision so that they can be certain that they have considered all the alternatives.

- Appointments are necessary and everyone is expected to arrive on time.

- Wait until you have established a relationship with your Dutch contacts before presenting them with gifts.

- Business dress in the Netherlands is fairly conservative, but it depends upon the profession.

- Business hours are usually from 8:30 AM to 5:30 PM on weekdays. Some banks have one night a week open for late customers. Most stores are open from 8:00 AM to 8:00 PM although some stores stay open even later.

KEY WORDS

Appointment (business)

Afspraak

@F-SPR@K

Business card

Zaken kaart

Z@-K@N K@RT

Meeting

Ontmoeting

@NT-M@-T@N

Marketing

Marketing

M@R-K@-T@N

Office	**Presentation**
Kantoor	Presentatie
K@N-T@R	PR@-S@N-T@-T@

Telephone

Telefoon

T@-L@-F@N

USEFUL PHRASES

I have an appointment.

Ik heb een afspraak.

ⓘK HⒺB ⓤhN ⓐhF-SPⓇⓐhK

My name is… (your name). Pleased to meet you.

Mijn naam is... Leuk u te ontmoeten.

MⓘN NⓐhM ⓘS…

LⓞⓤK ⓞⓞ Tⓤh ⓞNT-Mⓞⓞ́-TⓤhN

Here is my card.

Hier is mijn kaart.

HⒺEⓇ ⓘS MⓘN KⓐhⓇT

I need an interpreter.

Ik heb een tolk nodig.

ⓘK HⒺB ⓤhN TⓞK Nⓞ́-Dⓤh

Can you write your address for me?

Kan je jouw adres opschrijven voor mij?

K@N Y@ Y@ @-DR@'S
@P-SHR@-F@N F@R M@

Can you write your phone number?

Kan je jouw telefoonnummer opschrijven?

K@N Y@ Y@
T@-L@-F@N-N@-M@

This is my phone number.

Dit is mijn telefoonnummer.

D@T @S M@N
T@-L@-F@N-N@-M@

His / Her name is...

Zijn / Haar naam is...

Z@N / H@R N@M @S...

Good-bye.

Tot ziens.

T@T S@NS

PHRASEMAKER

I need...

Ik heb...

ⓘK HⒺB...

▶ **a computer**

een computer nodig

ⓤhN KⓄM-Pⓞⓞ-TⓊr NⓄ-Dⓤh

▶ **a copy machine**

een kopieermachine nodig

ⓤhN KⓄ-PⒺⒺ-ⒺR-MⓐhSHⒺⒺ-Nⓤh
NⓄ-Dⓤh

▶ **a conference room**

een vergaderruimte nodig

ⓤhN FⒺR-Hⓐh-Dⓤh-RⓐhM-Tⓤh NⓄ-Dⓤh

▶ **a fax machine**

een faxmachine nodig

ⓤhN FⓐhKS-Mⓐh-SHⒺⒺ-Nⓤh NⓄ-Dⓤh

▶ **an interpreter**

een tolk nodig

ⓤhN TⓄLK NⓄ-Dⓤh

▸ **a lawyer**

een advocaat nodig

ⓊⒽN ⒶⒽT-Ⓕ-Ⓞ-KⒶⒽT NⓄ-DⓊⒽ

▸ **a notary**

een notaris nodig

ⓊⒽN NⓄ-TⒶⒽ-RⒾS NⓄ-DⓊⒽ

▸ **a pen**

een pen nodig

ⓊⒽN PⒺN NⓄ-DⓊⒽ

▸ **stamps**

postzegels nodig

PⓄST-SⒶ-HⓊⒽLS NⓄ-DⓊⒽ

▸ **stationery**

een kantoorboekhandel nodig

ⓊⒽN KⒶⒽN-TⓄR-BⓄⓄK-HⒶⒽN-DⓊⒽL
NⓄ-DⓊⒽ

▸ **typing paper**

typ papier nodig

TⒺⒺP PⒶⒽ-PⒺⒺR NⓄ-DⓊⒽ

GENERAL INFORMATION

The Netherlands has a moderate maritime climate, with cool summers and mild winters. The coldest months are December through March; however, rain is likely all year round.

SEASONS

Spring

Lente

LĔN-Tᴜʰ

Summer

Zomer

ZŌ-Mᵁʳ

Autumn

Herfst

HĔᴿFST

Winter

Winter

VĬN-Tᵁʳ

THE DAYS

Monday

Maandag

M@N-D@

Tuesday

Dinsdag

D@NS-D@

Wednesday

Woensdag

W@NS-D@

Thursday

Donderdag

D@N-D@-D@

Friday

Vrijdag

FR@-D@

Saturday

Zaterdag

Z@-T@-D@

Sunday

Zondag

Z@N-D@

THE MONTHS

January	February
Januari	Februari
Y@N-Y@-ah-R€€	F@-BR@-ah-R€€

March	April
Maart	April
M@RT	@-PR@L

May	June
Mei	Juni
M①	Y@-N€€

July	August
Juli	Augustus
Y@-L€€	@-H@S-T@S

September	October
September	Oktober
S@P-T@M-B@r	@K-T@-B@r

November	December
November	December
N@-F@M-B@r	D@-S@M-B@r

COLORS

Black	**White**
Zwart	Wit
ZV@BT	V①T

Blue	**Brown**
Blauw	Bruin
BL@	BB@N

Gray	**Gold**
Grijs	Goud
HB①S	H@T

Orange	**Yellow**
Oranje	Geel
①-B@N-Y@	H@L

Red	**Green**
Rood	Groen
B①T	HB@N

Pink	**Purple**
Roze	Paars
B①-Z@	P@BS

NUMBERS

0	**1**	**2**	
nul	een	twee	
N◎◎L	ⒶN	TVⒶ	

3	**4**	**5**	**6**
drie	vier	vijf	zes
DRⒺⒺ	FⒺⒺR	FⒾF	ZⓔS

7	**8**	**9**	**10**
zeven	acht	negen	tien
ZⒶ-FⓊN	ⓐKT	NⒶ-HⓊN	TⒺN

11	**12**
elf	twaalf
ⓔLF	TVⓐLF

13	**14**
dertien	veertien
DⓔR-TⒺN	FⒺⒺR-TⒺN

15	**16**
vijftien	zestien
FⒾF-TⒺN	ZⓔS-TⒺN

17	**18**
zeventien	achttien
ZⒶ-FⓊN TⒺN	ⓐK-TⒺN

19
negentien
NA-HuhN-TEEN

20
twintig
TVIN-Tuh

30
dertig
DERB-Tuh

40
veertig
FEERB-Tuh

50
vijftig
FIF-Tuh

60
zestig
ZESS-Tuh

70
zeventig
ZA-VuhN-Tuh

80
tachtig
TahK-Tuh

90
negentig
NA-HuhN-Tuh

100
honderd
HON-DURT

1,000
duizend
Dow-ZuhNT

1,000,000
een miljoen
AN MIL-Yoon

DICTIONARY

Each English entry is followed by the Dutch spelling and then the EPLS Vowel Symbol System.

A

a, an een ⓤN

a lot veel FⓐL

able bekwaam Bⓤ K-Vⓐ M

accident ongeluk ⓄN-Hⓤh-LⓞⓞK

accommodation accomodatie ⓐh-KⓄ-Mⓐh-Dⓐh-Tⓔⓔ

account rekening Rⓐ-Kⓤh-NⓔⓔN

address adres ⓐh-DRⓔⓔS

admission toelating Tⓞⓞ-Lⓐh-TⓔⓔN

afraid bang Bⓐh N

after daarna Dⓐh R-Nⓐh

afternoon middag MⓄ-Dⓐh

agency agentschap ⓐh-Hⓔ NT-SHⓐh P

air-conditioning airconditioning ⓔ B-Kⓐh N-DⓄ-SHⓤh-NⓔⓔN

airline luchtvaartlijn Lⓞⓤ KT-Fⓐh BT-LⓄ N

126

airport luchthaven LOOKT-Hah-FuhN

aisle doorgang DOB-HahN

all alle ahL-Luh

all (everything) alles ahL-LuhS

almost bijna BOI-Nah

alone alleen ahL-LAN

also ook OK

always altijd ahL-TOT

ambulance ziekenwagen ZEE-KuhN-Vah-HuhN

American Amerikaans ah-MEE-BEE-KahNS

and en eN

another nog een NOH AN

anything om het even OM HeT A-FuhN

apartment appartement ahP-PahB-Tuh-MeNT

appetizers voorgerechten FOB-Huh-BeK-TuhN

apple appel ahP-PuhL

appointment afspraak ahF-SPBahK

April April ah-PBOL

arrival aankomst ahN-KOMST

ashtray asbak ahS-BahK

aspirin   aspirine   (ah)S-P(EE)-R(EE)-N(uh)

attention   aandacht   (ah)N-D(ah)KT

August   Augustus   (ow)-H(oo)S-T(ou)S

Australia   Australië   (ow)S-TR(ah)L-Y(uh)

Australian   Autralisch   (ow)S-TR(ah)-L(I)SH

author   auteur   (ow)-T(oo)R

automobile   auto   (ow)-T(O)

autumn   herfst   H(e)RFST

avenue   laan   L(ah)N

awful   afschuwelijk   (ah)F-SH(oo)-V(uh)-L(I)K

B

baby   baby   B(A)-B(EE)

babysitter   baby sitter   B(A)-B(EE) S(I)T-T(ur)

bacon   spek   SP(e)K

bad   slecht   SL(e)KT

bag   zak   Z(ah)K

baggage   bagage   B(ah)-H(ah)-SH(uh)

baked   gebakken   H(uh)-B(ah)K-K(uh)N

bakery   bakkerij   B(ah)-K(uh)-R(I)

banana   banaan   Bah-Nah'N

Band-Aid   verband   Fur-Bah'NT

bank   bank   Bah'NK

barber   kapper   Kah'P-Pur

bartender   barman   Bah'R-Mah'N

bath   bad   Bah'T

bathing suit   zwempak   SVe'M-Pah'K

bathroom   badkamers   Bah'T-Kah-Mur

battery   batterij   Bah-Tur-I

beach   strand   STRah'NT

beautiful   mooi   Moy

beauty shop   schoonheids sallon   SHO'N-HO'TS Sah-LO'N

bed   bed   Be'T

beef   rundvlees   Boo'NT-FLah'S

beer   bier   Bee'R

bellman   hotelediende   HO'T-e'L Bah-Dee'N-Duh

belt   riem   Bee'M

big   groot   HRO'T

bill   rekening   Bah'-Kuh-Nee'N

black   zwart   SV@RT

blanket   deken   D@-K@N

blue   blauw   BL@

boat   boot   B@T

book   boek   B@K

bookstore   boekhandel   B@K-H@N-D@L

border   grens   HR@NS

boy   jongen   Y@N-H@N

bracelet   armband   @BM-B@NT

brakes   remmen   B@M-M@N

bread   brood   BR@T

breakfast   ontbijt   @NT-B@T

broiled   geroosterd   H@-R@S-T@RT

brother   broer   BR@R

brown   bruin   BR@N

brush   borstel   B@R-ST@L

building   gebouw   H@-B@

bus   bus   B@S

bus station   busstation   B@S-ST@T-SH@N

bus stop   bushalte   B@SH-H@L-T@

business zaken Z@-K@N

butter boter B@'-T@

buy (to) koopen K@'-P@N

C

cab taxi T@K-S@

call (to) bellen B@'L-L@N

camera camera K@'-M@-R@

Canada Canada K@'-N@-D@

Canadian Canadees K@-N@-D@'S

candy snoep SN@P

car auto @-T@

carrot wortel V@'R-T@L

castle kasteel K@S-T@'L

cathedral kathedraal K@-T@-DR@'L

celebration viering F@'R-@N

center centrum S@N-TR@M

chair stoel ST@L

champagne champagne SH@M-P@N-Y@

change (money) wisselen V@'-S@-L@N

change (to)   veranding   FUH-RAN-DEN

cheap   goedkoop   HOOT-KOP

check (restaurant bill)   rekening   RA-KUH-NEN

cheers!   proost   PROST

cheese   kaas   KAHS

chicken   kip   KIP

child   kind   KENT

chocolate   chocolade   SHO-KO-LAH-DUH

church   kerk   KERK

cigar   sigaar   SEE-HAHR

cigarette   sigaret   SEE-HAH-RET

city   stad   STAHT

clean   schoon   SHON

close (to)   sluiten   SLOW-TUHN

closed   gesloten   HUHS-LO-TUHN

clothes   kleding   KLA-DEN

cocktail   cocktail   KOK-TAL

coffee   koffie   KO-FEE

cold (temperture)   koud   KOWT

comb   kam   KAHM

come (to) komen KŌ-MᵘʰN

company bedrijf Bᵘʰ-DRŌF

computer computer KOM-PYŌŌ-Tᵘʳ

concert concert KON-SᵉᵉRT

condom condoom KON-DŌM

conference conferentie KON-Fᵉᵉ-RᵉᵉN-TSᵉᵉ

conference room congres zaal KON-HRᵉᵉS ZᵃʰL

congratulations! gefeliciteerd
H̰ᵘʰ-FA-Lᵉᵉ-Sᵉᵉ-TᵉᵉRT

contraceptive voorbehoedsmiddel
FŌR-Bᵘʰ-HŌŌT-Mᵢ-DᵘʰL

copy machine kopieër apparaat
KŌ-PᵉᵉᵉR ᵃʰP-Pᵃʰ-RᵃʰT

corn mais MᵢS

cough medicine hoestdrankje HᵒᵒST-DRᵃʰNK-Yᵘʰ

cover charge entree ᵃʰN-TRA

crab krab KRᵃʰB

cream room ROM

credit card creditcard KRᵉ-DᵢT-KᵃʰRT

cup kopje KOP-Yᵘʰ

customs douane DŌŌ-ᵃʰ-Nᵘʰ

D

dance (to)   dansen   D@N-S@N

dangerous   gevaarlijk   H@-F@B-L@K

date (calender)   datum   D@-T@M

day   dag   D@

December   December   D@-S@M-B@

delicious   heerlijk   H@B-L@K

dentist   tandarts   T@NT-@BTS

deodorant   deodorant   D@-O-DO-B@NT

department store   warenhuis   V@-B@N-H@S

departure   vertrek   F@-TB@K

dessert   nagerecht   N@-H@-B@KT

detour   omweg   @M-W@H

diabetic   suikerpatient   S@-K@-P@-SH@NT

diarrhea   diarree   D@-@-B@

dictionary   woordenboek   V@B-D@N-B@K

dining room   eetzaal   @T-Z@L

dinner   diner   D@-N@

direction   richting   B@K-T@N

dirty   vuil   FOWL

disabled   gehandicapt   HUH-HAHN-DEE-KAHPT

discount   korting   KOR-TEEN

distance   afstand   AHF-STAHNT

doctor   dokter   DOK-TUR

document   document   DOH-KOO-MENT

dollar   dollar   DOH-LAHR

down   neer   NEER

downtown   down town   DOWN-TOWN

drink (beverage)   drankje   DRAHNK-YUH

drugstore   apotheek   AH-PO-TAHK

dry cleaner   stomerij   STOH-MUH-RIY

duck   eend   ANT

E

ear   oor   OR

ear drops   oor druppels   OR DROP-PUHLS

early   vroeg   FROOK

east   oosten   OS-TUHN

easy   makkelijk   MAHK-KUH-LUHK

eat (to)   eten   A-TUHN

egg   ei   I

egg (fried)   gebakken ei   HUH-BAHK-KUHN I

egg (scrambled)   roer ei   ROOR I

electricity   elektriciteit   A-LEK-TREE-SEE-TIT

elevator   lift   LEEFT

e-mail   e-mail   (same as in English)

embassy   ambassade   AHM-BAHS-SAH-DUH

emergency   noodgeval   NOT-HUH-FAHL

England   Engeland   EN-HUH-LAHNT

English   Engels   EN-HULS

enough!   genoeg   HUH-NOOH

entrance   ingang   EEN-HAHN

envelope   envelop   EN-FUH-LOP

evening   avond   AH-VONT

everything   alles   AHL-LES

excellent   uitstekend   OWT-STA-KUHNT

excuse me   pardon   PAHR-DON

exit   uitgang   OWT-HAHN

expensive   duur   DOOR

eye   oog   OH

eye drops oog druppels ⓞⒽ DRⓞP-PⓤLS

F

face gezicht HⓤH-ZⓘKT

far ver FⒺR

fast snel SNⒺL

father vader FⒶ-TⓊr

fax machine fax apparaat FⒶKS ⒶP-PⒶ-RⒶT

February Februari FⒺB-Rⓞⓞ-ⒶH-RⒺ

few weinig Vⓘ-NⓘH

film (movie) film FⓘLM

finger vinger FⒺN-HⓊr

fire brand BRⒶNT

first eerste ⒺRS-TⓤH

fish vissen FⓘS-SⓤN

flight vlucht FLⓞⓞKT

florist shop bloemen winkel BLⓞⓞ-MⓤN VⒺN-KⓤL

flower bloem BLⓞⓞM

food eten Ⓐ-TⓤN

foot voet FⓞⓞT

fork vork FⓞRK

french fries   patat   P(ah)-T(ah)T

fresh   vers   F(e)RS

Friday   Vrijdag   FR(I)-D(ah)

fried   bakken   B(ah)K-K(uh)N

friend   vriend / vriendin   FR(ee)NT / FR(ee)N-D(ee)N

fruit   vrucht   FR(oo)KT

funny   grappig   HR(ah)P-P(uh)H

G

gas station   pomp station   P(o)MP ST(ah)T-SH(o)N

gasoline   benzine   B(e)N-Z(ee)-N(uh)

gentleman   heer   H(ee)R

gift   cadeau   K(ah)-D(o)

girl   meisje   M(I)S-Y(uh)

glass (drinking)   glas   HL(ah)S

glasses (eye)   bril   BR(i)L

gloves   handschoen   H(ow)NTS-SH(oo)N

go   gaan   H(ah)N

gold   goud   H(ow)T

golf   golf   H(o)LF

golf course   golf baan   HOLF BahN

good   goed   HOT

good-bye   tot ziens   TOT SEENS

goose   gans   HahNS

grape   druif   DRaF

grateful   dankbaar   DahNKBahR

gray   grijs   HRiS

green   groen   HRooN

grocery store   supermarkt   Soo-PUr-MahRKT

group   groep   HRooP

guide   dirigeren   DEE-REE-HEE-RahN

H

hair   haar   HahR

hairbrush   borstel   BORST-STuhL

haircut   kapsel   KahP-SuhL

ham   ham   HahM

hamburger   hamburger   HahM-BUr-HUr

hand   hand   HahNT

happy   gelukkig   Huh-LooK-Kuh

have (to)   hebben   HEH-BuhN

he   hij   HI

head   hoofd   HOFT

headache   hoofdpijn   HOFT-PIN

health club (gym)   fitness centrum
    FIT-NehS   SEN-TRuhM

heart condition   hart valen   HahRT FAH-LuhN

heart   hart   HahRT

heat   hitte   HEET-Tuh

hello   hallo   HAH-LO

help! (emergency)   help!   HEHLP

here   hier   HEER

holiday   vakantie   FAH-KAHN-TSEE

hospital   ziekenhuis   ZEE-KuhN-HowS

hot dog   hot dog   HahT DahG

hotel   hotel   HO-TEHL

hour   uur   ooR

how   hoe   HOO

hurry up!   schiet op   SHEET OP

husband   echtgenoot   EKT-Huh-NOT

I

I ik ⓘK

ice ijs ⓘS

ice cream ijsje ⓘS-Yⓤㄴ

ice cubes ijs klontjes ⓘS KLⓄNT-YⓤㄴS

ill ziek ZⒺK

important belangrijk Bⓤㄴ-Lⓐㄴ-HฺฺฺⓡⓄK

indigestion indigestie ⓘN-DⒺ-HฺฺⓔⓢS-TⒺ

information informatie ⓘN-FⓄⓇ-Mⓐㄴ-TⒺ

internet cafe internet café (same as in English)

interpreter tolk TⓤㄴLK

J

jacket jasje YⓐㄴS-Yⓤㄴ

jam jam SHⓐM

January Januari Yⓐㄴ-Nⓞⓞ-ⓐㄴ-RⒺ

jewelry sieraden SⒺ-Rⓐㄴ-DⓤㄴN

jewelry store juwelier Yⓞⓞ-Vⓤㄴ-LⒺⓇ

job werk VⒺⓇK

juice sap SⓐㄴP

July   Juli   Y⊙⊙-L①

June   Juni   Y⊙⊙-N㊥

K

ketchup   ketchup   K㊤TCH-㊤P

key   sleutel   SL⊙-T㊤L

kiss   kus   K㊥S

knife   mes   M㊤S

know (to)   bekend zijn   B㊤-K㊤NT Z①N

L

ladies room   dames toilet   D㊐-M㊥S T㊍-L㊤T

lady   dame   D㊐-M㊤

lamb   lamsvlees   L㊐MS-FL㊐S

language   taal   T㊐L

large   groot   H̲R⊙T

late   laat   L㊐T

laundry   was   V㊐S

lawyer   advocaat   ㊐T-V⊙-K㊐T

left (direction)   links   L㊤NKS

leg   been   B㊐N

lemon   citroen   SEE-TROON

less   minder   MIN-DUr

letter   brief   BREEF

lettuce   sla   SLah

light   licht   LIKT

lips   lippen   LIP-Puhn

lipstick   lippenstift   LIP-Puhn-STIFT

little (amount)   beetje   BAT-Yuh

little (size)   klein   KLIN

live (to)   wonen   VO-Nuhn

lobster   kreeft   KRAFT

long   lang   Lahn

lost   verdwaald   FeB-DVahLT

love   liefde   LEEF-Duh

luck   geluk   Huh-LooK

luggage   bagage   Bah-Hah-SHuh

lunch   lunch   LooNCH

M

maid (at hotel)   dienstmeisje   DEENST-MI-SHuh

mail   post   POST

makeup   make up   MAK-uhP

man   man   MahN

manager   manager   Mā-Nuh-JUr

map   plattegrond   PLahT-Tuh-HRONT

March   Maart   MahRT

market   markt   MahRKT

matches   (light)   lucifers   Loo-Se-FeRS

May   Mei   MI

mayonnaise   mayonaisse   Mah-YO-NA-Suh

meal   maaltijd   MahL-TIT

meat   vlees   FLAS

meeting   vergadering   FeR-Hah-TUr-EEN

menu   kaart   KahRT

message   bericht   Buh-RIKT

milk   melk   MeLK

mineral water   mineraal water
   MEE-Nuh-RahL Vah-TUr

minute   minuut   Me-NooT

Miss   juffrouw   Yuh-FRow

mistake vergissing FĔB-HĬS-SĒN

misunderstanding misverstand MĬS-FŬ-STⓐNT

moment moment MŌ-MĔNT

Monday Maandag MⒶN-DⒶ

money geld HĔLT

month maand MⒶNT

monument monument MŌ-NŌŌ-MĔNT

more meer MⒶB

morning ochtend ŎK-TĔNT

mosque moskee MŎS-KⒶ

mother moeder MŌŌ-DŬ

mountain berg BĔBH

movies film FĬLM

Mr. Meneer MŬ-NĒB

Mrs. Mevrouw MŬ-FBŌW

museum museum MŌŌ-SⒶ-ŭM

mushrooms champignons SHⒶM-PĒ-ŎNS

music muziek MŌŌ-ZĒK

mustard mosterd MŎS-TŬBT

N

nail polish   nagel lak   NAH-HUHL LAHK

name   naam   NAHM

napkin   servet   SEHR-FEHT

near   dichtbij   DIKT-BI

neck   nek   NEHK

need (to)   nodig hebben   NO-DUH HEHB-BUHN

never   nooit   NOYT

newspaper   krant   KRAHNT

news stand   kiosk   KEEOSK

next time   volgende keer   FOL-HUHN-DUH KEER

night   nacht   NAHKT

nightclub   nightclub   NAHKT-KLUHB

no   nee   NA

no smoking   niet roken   NEET RO-KUHN

noon   middag   MI-DAH

north   noorden   NOR-DUHN

notary   notaris   NO-TAH-RIS

November   November   NO-VEHM-BUR

now   nu   NOO

number   nummer   NUH-MUR

nurse   verplegen   FER-PLA-HUHN

O

occupied   bezet   BUH-ZET

ocean   oceaan   O-SH-A-ahN

October   Oktober   OK-TO-BUR

officer   officier   O-FEE-SEER

oil   olie   O-LEE

omelet   omelet   O-MUH-LET

one-way (traffic)   een richtings   AN ROK-TENS

onion   ui   I

online   online   (same as in English)

open (to)   openen   O-PE-NUHN

opera   opera   O-PUR-ah

operator   operator   O-PUR-a-TOR

optician   opticien   OP-TEE-SHEN

orange (color)   oranje   O-RahN-Yuh

orange (fruit)   sinasappel   SEE-Nah-SahP-PuhL

order (to)   bestellen   BES-TE-LuhN

original   oorspronkelijk   OS-PRON-Kuh-Luhk

owner   eigenaar   I-Huh-Nahr

oysters   oesters   OOS-TUHS

P

package   pakketje   PahK-KAT-Yuh

pain   pijn   PIN

painting   schilderij   SHIL-DUH-I

paper   papier   Pah-PEER

parking lot   parkeer plaats   PahR-KEER PLahTS

partner (business)   partner   PahRT-NUr

party   feestje   FA-SHuh

passenger   passagier   PahS-Sah-HEER

passport   paspoort   PahS-PORT

pasta   pasta   PahS-Tah

pastry   gebak   Huh-BahK

pen   pen   PEN

pencil   potlood   PahT-LOT

pepper   peper   PA-PUr

perfume   parfum   PahR-FooM

person persoon PĒR-SŌN

pharmacist apotheker ah-PŌ-TĀ-KUr

pharmacy apotheek ah-PŌ-TĀK

phone book telefoonboek TĒ-Luh-FŌN-BooK

photo foto FŌ-TŌ

photographer fotograaf FŌ-TŌ-HRahF

pink roze RŌ-Zuh

plastic plastic PLĀS-TĪK

plate bord BORT

please alstublieft ahLS-Too-BLĒFT

pleasure plezier PLuh-ZĒR

police politie PŌ-LĒ-TSē

police station politie bureau PŌ-LĒ-TSē Boo-RŌ

pork varkensvlees FahR-KuhNS-FLāS

post office postkantoor PŌST-KahN-TOR

postcard briefkaart BRēF-KahRT

potato aardappel ahRT-ahP-Puhl

pregnant zwanger ZVahN-HUr

prescription voorgeschreven FŌR-Huhs-SHRā-Fuhn

price prijs PRĪS

problem   probleem   PROB-LAM

profession   beroep   Buh-ROOP

public   openbaar   O-PEN-BahR

public telephone   telefoon cel   TE-Luh-FON SEL

purple   paars   PahRS

purse   tas   TahS

Q

quality   kwaliteit   KWah-LEE-TIT

question   vraag   FRah

quickly   snel   SNEL

R

radio   radio   Bah-DEE-O

railroad   spoorweg   SPOR-VEH

rain   regen   BA-Huh N

rare (cooked)   rauw   Row

razor blades   scheermesjes   SHEER-MES-Yuh S

ready   klaar   KLahR

receipt   recept   BE-SEPT

recommend (to)   aanbevelen   ahN-Buh-FA-Luh N

red rood BⓞT

Repeat! Herhaal! HⓔB-HⓐL

reservation reservering BⒶ-SⓔB-FⓔB-ⒺN

restaurant restaurant BⓔS-Tⓞw-BⓐNT

return terug geven Tⓔ-BⓞⓞH HⒶ-FⓤN

rice (cooked) rijst BⓘST

rich rijk BⓘK

right (correct) juist YⓞⓞST

right (direction) rechts BⓔKTS

road weg VⓔH

room kamer Kⓐ-MⓊⓇ

round trip rond reis BⓞNT BⓘS

S

safe (hotel) klein KLⓘN

salad salade Sⓐ-Lⓐ-Dⓤⓗ

sale verkoop FⓔB-KⓞP

salmon zalm Zⓐ-LⓤⓗM

salt zout ZⓞwT

sandwich broodje BBⓞT-Yⓤⓗ

Saturday Zaterdag Zⓐ-TⓊⓇ-Dⓐ

sculpture beeldhouwerk BALT-How-VeRK

seafood zee vruchten ZA FRooK-TuhN

season kruiden KRow-DuhN

seat stoel STooL

secretary secretaresse Se-KRe-Tah-Re-Suh

section sectie SeK-TSee

September September SeP-TeM-BUr

service dienst DeeNST

several verscheidene FeR-SHI-Duh-Nuh

shampoo shampoo SHaM-PO

sheets (bed) lakens Lah-KuhNS

shirt overhemd O-FUr-HeMT

shoe schoen SHON

shoe store schoenen winkel SHO-NuhN-VeeN-KuhL

shopping center winkel centrum
VeeN-KuhL SeN-TRuhM

shower douchen Doo-SHuhN

shrimp garnaal HahB-NahL

sick ziek ZeeK

sign (display) bord BOBT

signature handtekening H@NDT-T@-K@-N@N

Silence! Stilte! ST@L-T@

single vrijgezel FR@-H@-Z@L

single (unmarried) ongehuwd @N-H@-H@T

sir meneer M@-N@R

sister zus Z@S

size omvang @M-F@N

skin huid H@T

skirt rok B@K

sleeve mouw M@

slowly langzaam L@N-Z@M

small klein KL@N

smile (to) glimlachen HL@M-L@-K@N

smoke (to) roken B@-K@N

soap zeep Z@P

socks sokken S@K-K@N

some een beetje @N B@T-Y@

something iets @TS

sometimes soms S@MS

soon   snel   SNĚL

sorry (I am)   het spijt mij   HĚT SPĪT MĪ

soup   soep   SOOP

south   zuidelijk   ZOW-DUH-LUHK

souvenir   aandenken   AHN-DAN-KUHN

Spanish   Spaans   SPAHNS

speciality   speciliteit   SPA-SHAH-LEE-TĪT

speed   snelheid   SNĚL-HĪT

spoon   lepel   LA-PUHL

sport   sport   SPORT

spring (season)   lente   LĚN-TUH

stairs   trap   TRAP

stamp   postzegel   POST-ZA-HUHL

station   station   STAHT-SHON

steak   biefstuk   BEEF-STUK

steamed   gestoomd   HUH-STOMT

Stop!   Stop!   STOP

store   winkel   VEEN-KUHL

storm   storm   STORM

straight ahead   rechtdoor   REKT-DOR

strawberry aardbei ahRT-BI

street straat STRaht

string koord KORT

subway metro MA-TRO

sugar suiker Sow-KUr

suit (clothes) pak PahK

suitcase koffer KOF-FUr

summer zomer ZO-MUr

sun zon ZON

Sunday Zondag ZON-Dah

sunglasses zonnebril ZON-Nuh-BREL

suntan lotion zonnebrand ZON-Nuh-BRahNT

supermarket supermarkt Soo-PUr-MahRKT

surprise verrassen FeR-RahS-SuhN

sweet zoet ZooT

swim (to) zwemmen ZVeM-MuhN

swimming pool zwembad ZVeM-BahT

synagogue synagoge SEE-Nah-HO-Huh

T

table tafel T@-F@L

tampons tampon T@M-P@N

tape (sticky) plakband PL@K-B@NT

tax belasting B@-L@S-T@N

taxi taxi T@K-S@

tea thee T@

telephone telefoon T@-L@-F@N

television televisie T@-L@-F@-S@

temperature temperatuur T@M-P@-@-T@R

temple tempel T@M-P@L

tennis tennis T@N-N@S

tennis court tennisbaan T@N-N@S-B@N

thank you! dank je! D@NK Y@

that dat D@T

the de, het D@ / H@T

theater (movie) bioscoop B@-@-SK@P

there daar D@R

they zij Z@

this dit D@T

thread draad DR@hT

throat keel K@L

Thursday Donderdag D@N-D@-D@

ticket kaartje K@hBT-Y@h

tie vastbinden F@hST-B@N-D@hN

time tijd T@T

tip (gratuity) fooi F@y

tire wiel V@L

tired moe M@

toast (bread) toast T@ST

tobacco tabak T@h-B@hK

today vandaag F@hN-D@

toe teen T@N

together samen; S@h-M@hN

toilet toilet, w.c. TW@h-L@T

toilet paper toilet papier T@y-L@T P@h-P@R

tomato tomaat T@-M@hT

tomorrow morgen M@R-H@hN

toothache kiespijn K@S-P@N

toothbrush tandenborstel T@hN-D@hN-B@RS-T@hL

toothpaste   tandpasta   TahNT-PahS-Tah

toothpick   tandenstoker   TahN-DahN-STO-KUr

tour   tour   TOR

tourist   toerist   TOO-RiST

tourist office   toesisten bureau
TOO-RiS-TuhN BOO-RO

towel   handoek   HahN-DOOK

train   trein   TRiN

travel agency   reis bureau   RiS BOO-RO

traveler's check   reis cheque   RiS SHeK

trip   struikelen   STROW-KUh-LuhN

trousers   broek   BROOK

trout   forel   FO-ReL

truth   waarheid   VahRB-HiT

Tuesday   Dinsdag   DeeNS-Dah

U

umbrella   paraplu   Pah-Rah-PLOO

understand (to)   begrijpen   Buh-HRi-PuhN

underwear   ondergoed   ON-DUr-HOOT

United Kingdom Vereningde Koninkrijk
F®-R®-N①H-D⑩ K⓪-N€€N-KR①K

United States Verenigde Staten
F®-R®-N①H-D⑩ STⓐT-⑩N

university universiteit ⓞⓞ-N€€-F⑩-S€€-T①T

up omhoog ⓞM-H⓪H

urgent dringend DRⓐN-⑩NT

V

vacant vrij FR①

vacation vakantie Fⓐ-KⓐN-TS€€

valuable waardevol VⓐR-D⑩-FⓞL

value waarde VⓐR-D⑩

vanilla vanille Vⓐ-N€€L-Y⑩

veal kalfsvlees KⓐLFS-FLⓐS

vegetables groente HRⓞⓞN-T⑩

view kijken K①-K⑩N

vinegar azijn ⓐ-Z①N

voyage reizen R①-Z⑩N

W

Wait! Wachttijd! VⓐKT-T①T

waiter / waitress kelner / serveerster
K@L-N@ / S@B-V@B-ST@

want (to) willen V@L-L@N

wash (to) wassen V@S-S@N

Watch out! Kijk uit! K@K @T

water water V@-T@

watermelon watermeloen V@-T@-M@-L@N

weather weer V@B

Wednesday Woensdag V@NS-D@

week week V@K

weekend weekend V@K-@NT

welcome welkom V@L-K@M

well done (cooked) gaar H@B

west west V@ST

wheelchair rolstoel B@L-ST@L

When? Wanneer? V@N-N@B

Where? Waar ? V@B

Which? Welke? V@L-K@

white wit V@T

Who? Wie V@

Why? Waarom! Vah'-BooM

wife vrouw FRow

wind wind VIND

window raam Bah-M

wine wijn VIN

wine list wijn kaart VIN Kah-BT

winter winter VIN-TUr

with met MeT

woman vrouw FRow

wonderful wonderbaarlijk VIN-DUr-Bah'B-LuhK

world wereld VEEB-uhLT

wrong fout FowT

XYZ

year jaar Yah-B

yellow geel HAL

yes ja Yah

yesterday gisteren HEE'-STuh-BuhN

you jij YI

zipper rits (sluiting) BITS

zoo dierentuin (beginsel) DEE'-BuhN-TuhN

THANKS!

The nicest thing you can say to anyone in any language is "Thank you." Try some of these languages using the incredible EPLS Vowel Symbol System.

Spanish	French
GR**ah**´-S**EE**-**ah**S	M**ĕ**R-S**EE**

German	Italian
D**ah**´N-K**uh**	GR**ah**´T-S**EE**-**ĕ**

Japanese	Chinese
D**O**´-M**O**	SH**EE****ĕ** SH**EE****ĕ**

Swedish	Portuguese
T**ah**K	**O**-BR**EE**-G**ah**-D**O**

Arabic	Greek
SH**oo**-KR**ah**N	**e**F-H**ah**-R**EE**-ST**O**

Hebrew	Russian
T**O**-D**ah**	SP**ah**-S**EE**-B**ah**

Swahili	Dutch
ah-S**ah**N-T**A**	D**ah**NK **oo**

Tagalog	Hawaiian
S**ah**-L**ah**-M**ah**T	M**ah**-H**ah**-L**O**

INDEX

NOTES

QUICK REFERENCE PAGE

Hello	**Hello**
Hoi	**Hallo** (polite)
H(oy)	H(ah)-L(o)

How are you?

Hoe gaat het?

H(oo) H(ah)T H(e)T

Yes	**No**
Ja	Nee
Y(ah)	N(a)

Please

Alstublieft

(ah)LS-T(oo)-BL(ee)FT

Thank you (informal)	**Thank you very much** (formal)
Dank u	Dank u wel
D(ah)NK (oo)	D(ah)NK (oo) V(e)L

Excuse me / I'm sorry	**Help!**
Pardon	Help!
P(ah)R-D(o)N	H(e)LP

I don't understand!

Ik begrijp het niet!

(i)K B(uh)-HR(i)P H(e)T N(ee)T

166